Your Essential Guide to

# EFFECTIVE REFLECTIVE PRACTICE

Your Essential Guide to

# EFFECTIVE REFLECTIVE PRACTICE

## Improving Practice through Self-Reflection and Writing

Christian van Nieuwerburgh

David Love

Sage

1 Oliver's Yard
55 City Road
London EC1Y 1SP

2455 Teller Road
Thousand Oaks
California 91320

Unit No 323-333, Third Floor, F-Block
International Trade Tower
Nehru Place, New Delhi – 110 019

8 Marina View Suite 43-053
Asia Square Tower 1
Singapore 018960



Editor: Jai Seaman
Editorial assistant: Becky Oliver
Production editor: Martin Fox
Copyeditor: Jane Fricker
Proofreader: Derek Markham
Marketing manager: Fauzia Eastwood
Cover design: Shaun Mercier
Typeset by: C&M Digitals (P) Ltd, Chennai, India
Printed and bound by CPI Group (UK) Ltd,
Croydon, CR0 4YY

**Library of Congress Control Number: 2024937129**

**British Library Cataloguing in Publication data**

A catalogue record for this book is available from the British Library

ISBN 978-1-5296-2093-1
ISBN 978-1-5296-2092-4 (pbk)

Christian writes:

To Cathia and Christian Jr, with love and admiration.

David writes:

To Alba, Rowen, Tom, Sara, Ben, Bernie, Pam and Digby – for being a constant source of joy and inspiration.

# CONTENTS

# ONLINE RESOURCES

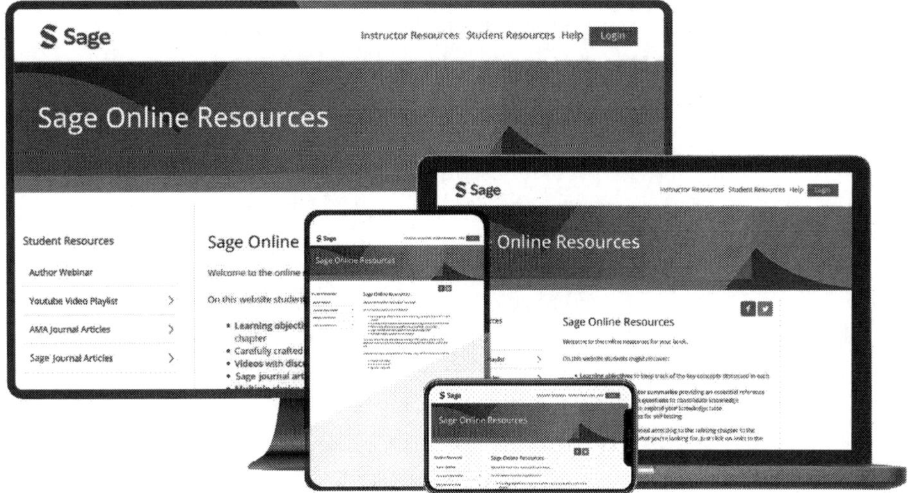


*Your Essential Guide to Effective Reflective Practice* is supported by a wealth of online resources, which are available to access at:
**https://study.sagepub.com/nieuwerburghlove1e.**

## STUDENT RESOURCES

Templates to provide students with a clear example of expectations and structure, guiding them in their own work:

- Template for reflective practice plan.
- Template for reflective writing, including worked examples.

Assessment to give students a concrete understanding of the criteria and standards required, helping them to better prepare and perform in their evaluations:

- Examples of marked assignments with marking guide.

Colour versions of figures are available:

- 9.3 Revised inauthentic leadership cartoon
- 9.4 Image created by David Love to reflect on his Dracula-like inner critic
- 9.5 A collage created by David Love focusing on moving forward in his career
- 9.6 Arranging cards
- 9.7 Painting over cards
- 9.9 Face or mask?
- 10.1 The place of art in professional practice
- A3.6 Annotated image suggested by original doodle
- A3.8 Modelling
- A3.9 Modelling completed
- A3.11 Creating impact through cartooning.

## LECTURER RESOURCES

PowerPoint Decks to help lecturers organise their teaching in a clear, logical sequence, making it easier for students to follow along:

- Overview of the Effective Reflective Practice framework
- Assessment briefing on the Effective Reflective Practice framework

# ABOUT THE AUTHORS

**Prof. Christian van Nieuwerburgh** (PhD) is an academic, consultant and executive coach. He is Professor of Coaching and Positive Psychology at the Centre for Positive Health Sciences at RCSI University of Medicine and Health Sciences (Ireland) and Consulting Professor for Growth Coaching International, a provider of coach training and consultancy for the education sector. In recognition of his contributions to the fields of positive psychology and coaching, he is Principal Fellow of the Centre for Wellbeing Science at the Melbourne Graduate School of Education of the University of Melbourne (Australia) and Honorary CollectivEd Fellow of the Carnegie School of Education at Leeds Beckett University (UK).

Christian was born in Lebanon to a Belgian father and Japanese mother. He grew up in Beirut, attending the American Community School there before completing a BA in English Literature and then an MA in Shakespeare Studies at the American University of Beirut (Lebanon). He completed a PhD in Elizabethan Drama at the Shakespeare Institute of the University of Birmingham (UK) and an MSc in Psychology at the University of East London (UK).

In his varied professional life, Christian has worked as a taxi driver, waiter, box office assistant, marketing officer, bookseller, business development manager, assistant librarian, journalist, translator and academic. In England, he worked for the Royal Shakespeare Company, local authorities in England (Warwickshire County Council and Essex County Council), Waterstones, Henley Business School of the University of Reading (UK) and the School of Psychology at the University of East London (UK).

Christian is a certified executive coach through the European Mentoring and Coaching Council (Master Practitioner) and the International Coaching Federation (Professional Certified Coach). Christian is well published in the academic literature on the topics of coaching and positive psychology. He has authored, co-authored and edited numerous books: *Coaching in Education: Getting Better Results for Students, Educators and Parents* (2012); *An Introduction to Coaching Skills: A Practical Guide* (2014, 2016, 2020); *Coaching in Professional Contexts* (2016); *Coaching Educativo* (2016, with Andrea Giraldez-Hayes); *Coaching in Islamic Culture* (2017, with Raja'a Allaho); *The Leader's Guide to Coaching in Schools* (2018, with John Campbell); *Advanced Coaching Practice* (2019, with David Love); and *From Surviving to Thriving: A Student's Guide to Feeling and Doing Well at University* (2022, with Paige Williams). He enjoys writing and is currently working on books on radical listening, Zen and the art of coaching, and coaching in higher education.

Christian is passionate about the integration of coaching and positive psychology to improve outcomes and enhance wellbeing in educational, health and corporate settings. He regularly speaks at global conferences and has given presentations and delivered training in Europe, the US, South America, the Middle East, Africa, Asia, Australia and New Zealand. He enjoys spending time with family, travelling, writing and riding his Harley Davidson. He is riding some of the greatest motorcycle roads of the world. Follow Christian on his motorcycle adventures on Instagram (@coachonamotorcycle) and on his website (coachonamotorcycle.com).

**David Love** is a qualified and experienced leadership coach who works with senior and middle managers in the UK National Health Service, local government and other public services. He has extensive experience of organisational, leadership and management development and was a senior manager himself in further education for many years. Other past lives have included roles as a youth worker, an advice worker, a community worker, a teacher of English for Speakers of Other Languages, a communication and race equalities consultant and a university teacher. David is also a trained and experienced coach supervisor, working with individual coaches, networks of coaches and in-house coaching cadres. As a coach educator he designs and facilitates advanced coaching skills workshops. He views coaching and supervision as essentially forms of facilitated reflective practice.

After a period of 'academic fatigue' at school and higher education David went on to gain a B.Ed. as a mature student and then an MBA with the Open University. He holds an ILM Level 7 Diploma in Executive Coaching and Leadership Mentoring and Henley Business School's Professional Certificate in Coaching.

David is an art-based practitioner, bringing the creation of images and cartoons into his coaching and supervision activities and believing strongly in the power of creative methods for enabling people to generate the deep insights and learning which underpin personal and systemic change. He is one of the first coaches to complete the pioneering art-based coaching qualification, achieving the award of the Diploma in Art-based Coaching from the Association of Coaching. The creation of visual images through collaging and cartooning has long been a feature of David's private life where, for example, he enjoys creating with and for his two young granddaughters. In addition, David is the 'resident cartoonist' for the Association for Coaching's *Coaching Perspectives* magazine.

David is deeply committed to working to improve outcomes for citizens by enabling senior managers to become better leaders through coaching. He is particularly interested in the place of reflective practice in improving personal impact and performance, seeing coaching as a highly effective way of blending organisational priorities with leadership learning. David sees this work as encompassing leaders' responsibilities for making a difference with the 'big issues' facing humanity such as poverty, inclusion and the climate catastrophe. He works to build clients' capacity to self-coach and use coaching approaches with their colleagues as one way of building cultures where individual and team reflective practice contributes to improved service provision and business operations.

As an author, David collaborated with Christian to write *Advanced Coaching Practice: Inspiring Change in Others* (2019). He has also contributed pieces about the use of creative methods in coaching to *WeCoach: Coaching Tools and Techniques* (2022, 2023). Other publications include: *You've Got to Laugh: Cartooning in Coaching and Supervision* (*Coaching Perspectives*, April 2023); *How Can I Use GROW to Help My Coaching Clients? Insight Guide No. 7* (Henley Business School, 2019); *Coaching* (NHS Improvement, 2017); and *A Short Guide to Workplace Coaching Conversations* (NHS Improvement, 2017).

For Henley Business School, David designed and filmed 'Creative Techniques in Coaching', a series of ten short videos, with an accompanying workbook (2020). He is also a regular contributor to webinars and podcasts such as: 'Are You Having A Laugh – Cartooning in Coaching?' (Association for Coaching's Creative Festival, April 2024); 'Achieving the State of Flow' (Brain Fuel webinar, 2022); and 'How Can Coaching Help Me To Be More Creative?' (British Psychological Society's Special Interest Group in Coaching Psychology podcast, 2021).

David is a committed lifelong learner who continues to be intrigued by human beings, their relationships with each other and the world. For many years he has seen his own reflective practice habit as central to his continuing professional and personal development and has adopted an art-based approach which he uses routinely to explore topics related to his work and life.

# PROLOGUE

## WHY CHRISTIAN WANTED TO WRITE THIS BOOK

When each of us is living our best lives, I believe that we are better at looking after each other. Reflective practice is an opportunity for people to take a step back from the busy-ness, ugliness, excitement, noise or dullness of everyday life. Human beings are uniquely able to reflect not only on the present, but also the past and the future. This very human ability allows us to be more intentional about what we want for our own futures whilst also thinking about our desired impact on others.

Having grown up in Beirut, a city devastated by conflict and then living my entire adult life with conflicts taking place in different parts of the world, I am committed to exploring how individuals can make things better for themselves and others. To change the world is an impossible dream – but we each make small changes to the ways that we live and interact with others. If each of us is more intentional about how we live our own lives, we are more likely to experience greater levels of wellbeing. And if we are having our basic needs met and feeling more positive about our lives, we are more likely to be interested in the lives and wellbeing of others.

I have had a long-standing curiosity about human beings at their best – always fascinated by how kind, considerate and inspiring humans can be. That led me to make a career transition into academia to study human beings at their best. By engaging with the emerging fields of coaching and positive psychology, I sought to understand and study the conditions that would encourage people to be kind, considerate and inspiring. Learning about coaching, teaching it, being coached, coaching others, and supervising coaches have only increased my faith in the essential tendency towards goodness in human beings. As far as I can tell, most people are trying to do the right thing. Many hundreds of hours of coaching conversations back this up.

This is how I started to think that the process of reflective practice can have a role to play. But there are already reflective practice models out there. What was the need for a *new* framework? David Love and I wanted to highlight the importance of *positive intention* as the starting point for reflective practice. In other words, the practice should lead to better outcomes. We thought it was important to emphasise that the reflective practitioner's attention should be on the *impact on others,* rather than simply on a notion of 'self-improvement'. And we are convinced that reflective practice should *enhance* wellbeing rather than detract from it. We call for greater self-compassion when engaging in reflective practice and raised awareness of the wellbeing of those who are impacted by the professional. The real question driving this book is not 'how can we live better?' but 'how can we live better *together?*'

Another incentive for me to take on this project was the opportunity to work with my good colleague and friend, David Love. We enjoyed being co-authors on another book for SAGE, *Advanced Coaching Practice*. That process was thought-provoking, fun and enriching. I learnt so much about the topic through the process of thinking and writing with David.

## WHY DAVID WANTED TO WRITE THIS BOOK

Reflecting is about pressing the pause button and taking time out to make sense of where things are at. That might be the sole purpose. Simply to take stock. Additionally, the purpose might be to gain insights about how to move forward or make changes, particularly in a professional context where we want to perform at our best in the service of others. However, while creating an action plan might be a valuable outcome from some reflective activities, that is by no means the only benefit of reflective practice, which can have, for example, profound insights for our self-awareness, identity and wellbeing.

I am a person with an extremely strong preference for a reflective learning style, coupled with an inwardly focused approach for recharging my batteries. As a result, in writing this book I want to explore the quality of the ways we enact that pause for the purposes of reflection. *How* we enter the pause feels important. This is not about grabbing five minutes out of the hustle and bustle of a busy life to do a quick review of where things have got to before jumping back into the fray. Rather, the pausing needs to be a positive, deliberate action, implemented with the intent of truly taking time out for ourselves and creating an appropriate space for deep reflection in the particular ways that work best for each of us. How we do this will be influenced by, amongst other things, our backgrounds, experiences, preferences and passions, which all come together to create the optimal conditions for effective reflection to take place. I want this book to be a contribution to enabling you, the reader, to make your own decisions about the most effective approaches you can come up with for developing and sustaining a reflective practice habit.

For you to find your own effective reflective practices it feels essential to first have a core framework for creating and embedding the habit, as well as for capturing and recording the outcomes. I want this book to provide that strong foundation, from which it is then possible for you to incorporate any adaptations which personalise your reflective practice approach. Just as the core framework can be adapted in this way, your personal adaptations may also evolve over time to accommodate new interests or circumstances.

Over my years as an educator (of young people, leaders and coaches) I have seen how learners' capacity to do reflective practice well, and to write about reflective practice cogently, does not always come to people easily. Indeed, in my own career and life I have had to learn how to be effective in my own reflective practice and in getting my reflections down in print. For example, I have frequently found a tendency for professionals to focus purely on the facts of a situation, rather than the emotions those facts stimulate, the impact those emotions generate and the knock-on effects to relationships with others. I want this book to make a contribution to sharpening up both the 'doing' and the 'writing up' of reflective practice across a wide range of professional fields.

As an artist and cartoonist I want to explore the power of playfulness in Effective Reflective Practice. Perhaps counterintuitively, reflection is not just about *thinking*. The most powerful reflective outcomes often arise from creative activities like painting, poetry and music, which tap into how we experience and *feel* about a topic. For example, starting the reflective process with a mindfulness or visualisation exercise is a very effective way of creating that all-important initial pause and freeing the mind from focusing on thoughts. I am keen for this book to encourage you to engage in serious play as a way of providing radically different lenses through which to reflect on matters of importance in your work and life.

Finally, my co-author, Christian and I have a long-standing and strong relationship which has built up over many years and has profound significance for me. In 2019, we wrote and published a book together about our mutual professional passion, coaching. The experience of researching, thinking and writing together involved many thought-provoking, humorous and sometimes appropriately challenging conversations around real or virtual flipcharts covered in words, diagrams and sketches in myriad colours. I am eager for this, our next publishing venture, to replicate the same excitement of reflecting and learning together about how to be an effective reflective practitioner. I know for certain this experience will stretch my professional, and personal, thinking and capabilities in the service of others – and will involve a great deal of fun!

# ACKNOWLEDGEMENTS

## CHRISTIAN AND DAVID WRITE

First, we are grateful to you, the reader. Without you, this book would have no purpose.

Second, we thank all the interviewees who graciously gave their time to talk about their experiences and understanding of reflective practice:

Nick Andrew and Tanya Hinton, Artists

Daraius Cooper, Cranial Osteopath

Kate Cuthbertson, Social Worker, Practice Educator and Supervisor

Prof. Ashley Duggan, Social Scientist and Communication Expert

Di Henning, Senior Consultant and Coach Supervisor

Dr Nelly Nyugen, Executive Coach and Leadership Expert

Prof. Ciaran O'Boyle, Director of the Centre for Positive Health Sciences

Dr Jummy Okoya, Academic and Interim Dean of Office for Institutional Equity.

Each of them was invited to participate as a role model of someone who uses reflective practice effectively in their professional capacity whilst also integrating it positively into their personal lives. They were generous with their time and insights.

Third, we are grateful to the incredibly supportive team at SAGE publishers, particularly Jai Seaman, Commissioning Editor; Becky Oliver, Editorial Assistant; Martin Fox, Production Editor; Jane Fricker, Copyeditor; and Derek Markham, Proofreader. This book would not have been possible without their belief, ongoing support and encouragement. We are appreciative and proud of our association with SAGE.

## CHRISTIAN WRITES

It is an incredible privilege to have the opportunity to acknowledge and appreciate people in this way. This list is necessarily selective because I have learnt so much through my interactions with so many people.

It seems appropriate to start by acknowledging my educators. My first grade teacher, Nancy Reynolds at the American Community School of Beirut, has had a lifelong impact on me by simply including me. The teachings of Dr George Khairallah and Dr Jean-Marie Cook at the American University of Beirut were foundational and conversations with them inspired me to develop my critical thinking. I am grateful to them and all the academics at AUB whose commitment to the education of students was steadfast despite enormous challenges. Later, as I worked on my PhD at the Shakespeare Institute of the University of Birmingham, I had the good fortune of being supervised by a world-leading specialist in Elizabethan and Jacobean drama, Dr Martin Wiggins. He put his heart and soul into supporting his doctoral students. Dr Jim Knight has been an inspiring educator and mentor to me. He has taught me how much can be achieved by focusing on good work, having strong convictions and approaching people with kindness.

During my years working for the education department of Warwickshire County Council, I was fortunate to learn from amazing facilitators and teachers. Sue Herdman, Mary Johnson and Miles Tandy showed me how to bring a human touch to teaching and learning. Watching them deliver workshops was an important part of my own professional learning. Although I did not fully appreciate it at the time, they were living examples of reflective practitioners who continually sharpen their practice because they care so deeply about the outcomes for their clients.

In my academic career, I am grateful to Prof. Anthony Grant and Prof. Jonathan Passmore for their support and mentorship. As leading figures in the field of coaching psychology, I was inspired by their work and their generosity of spirit. During my time at the School of Psychology at the University of East London, I was fortunate to work with colleagues who were deeply committed to our students and what we taught. I am particularly grateful to my colleagues Dr Kirsty Gardiner, Dr Rona Hart, Dr Kate Hefferon, Dr Itai Ivtzan, Dr Hanna Kampman, Dr Ho Law, Dr Tim Lomas, Dr Ana Paula Nacif, Julia Papworth, William Pennington, Dr Nash Popovic, Dr Sok-Ho Trinh, Cecilia Yardley and Dr Julia Yates.

During my time at Henley Business School of the University of Reading, I learnt so much from my colleagues as we taught on the MSc in Coaching and Behavioural Change. I would like to particularly mention Prof. Patricia Bossons, Prof. Alison Hardingham, Ann James, Denis Sartain and Tracy Sinclair. We created positive learning environments together.

I am so grateful to be part of the Centre for Positive Health Sciences at RCSI University of Medicine and Health Sciences in Dublin. My colleagues are incredibly supportive and encouraging. I am grateful to Lucy Airs, Dr Jolanta Burke, Dr Elaine Byrne, Stephen Campbell, Marina Iglesias Cans, Dr Mary Collins, Jennifer Donnelly, Dr Pádraic Dunne, Louise Foott, Aine Garvey, Miriam Holden, Branislav Kaleta, Justin Laiti, Croia Loughnane, Dr Trudy Meehan, Dr Roisin O'Donovan, Ciara Scott, Suzanne Sullivan and Annette Sweeney. Working with them is a joyful experience.

Alongside my academic role, I have been lucky enough to be part of the leadership team at Growth Coaching International. I am grateful to my colleagues on the leadership team, Chris Munro, Debbie Knoke and Claudia Owad and members of the GCI Board: Vicky Campbell and Roy Ditmarsch. We are an organisation full of people who are deeply committed to supporting educators and it has been such a pleasure and a privilege to be part of the team which includes Jan Alen, Lizzie Bayliss, Susan Bentley, Marisa Burda, Ben Calleja, Lucy Carroll, Viv Cherry, Mandy Dunn, David Ellery, Mandy Fisher, Jackie Frankland, Marian Grant, Cath Grealy, Marilyn Gwilliam, Robert Hadchiti, Roween Higgie, Jan Hill, Georgina Holloway, Tom Hullena, Jess Joils, Dr Nicky Knight, Emma Kriketos, Debbie Lowe, Andrew MacDonald-Brown, Dr Julie Mathews, Tammy McCartney, Paul Meacock, Kath Morwitch, Jason Pascoe, Grant O'Sullivan, Sophie Paterson, Tima Pechous, David Price, Richard Reid, Sue Richards, Gray Ryan, Edna Sackson, Julie Schumacher, Theresa Sheehan, Brenda Sinclair-Jones, Dan Steele, Sonja Stubbs-Mills, Av Swami, Sharon Taylor, Anne Tonkin, Maria Tsavaris, Penny Verdich, Debbie Ward and Melinda Zanetich.

I learn so much through co-writing with others. I am grateful for my time with Raja'a Allaho working on the ground-breaking book, *Coaching in Islamic Culture*. The experience was full of learning and insights. Working with Dr Andrea Giraldez-Hayes on *Coaching Educativo* was an instructive and joyful experience. Collaborating with Dr Paige Williams on the book *From Surviving to Thriving* was a positive and uplifting experience, even in the midst of a pandemic.

I have been lucky throughout my professional life to have empowering leaders who encouraged me to pursue more of my potential. I am particularly grateful to Barbara Brown, my manager at Warwickshire County Council, who saw potential in me that I did not; Prof. Aneta Tunariu, Dean of the School of Psychology at the University of East London, who was a role model of graceful dignity and resilience; John Campbell, Founding Director of Growth Coaching International, a passionate leader and trusted mentor who has become a lifelong friend; Prof. Ciaran O'Boyle at the Centre for Positive Health Sciences at RCSI University of Medicine and Health Sciences, an inspiring role model of a visionary leader who is kind and warm-hearted.

My reflective practice depends on having a network of supportive, thoughtful and inspiring colleagues that I am able to reach out to for conversations and advice. I would like to thank the following people for being part of an enriching network of friends and colleagues: Margaret Barr, who is an exemplar of the 'coaching way of being'; Dr Robert Biswas-Diener, who is an inspiring colleague, respected thought leader and valued friend; Prof. Ilona Boniwell, who is an inspirational leader and trusted colleague; Prof. Ashley Duggan, who is able to connect people and ideas; Prof. Suzy Green, who inspires through her wisdom and zest for life; Dr Diego Hangartner, who teaches through his presence; Prof. Andrew Hobson, who is a trusted thinking partner; Dr Aaron Jarden, who seamlessly combines rigour and fun; Prof. Rachel Lofthouse, who is deeply committed to doing the right thing; Sander Markiet, who is an inspiring thought partner; Dr Nell Nyugen, who combines a passion for change with kindness and humility; Prof. Lindsay Oades, who is a visionary leader; Dr Jummy Okoya, who is a model of passionate determination; Brittany Rehal-Singh, who is an inspiring educator and changemaker; Wendy-Ann Smith, who is committed to making things better; Prof. Michael Steger, who gracefully combines great wisdom, humour and humility; and Prof. Bob Thomson, who has taught me so much about non-attachment.

My family is a source of meaning, joy and love. I am grateful to my late parents, Arthur J. van Nieuwerburgh and Tsuyu Tsuchida, for giving me a chance; to the love of my life, Cathia Jenainati, for being the ideal partner; and to my beloved son, Christian A. van Nieuwerburgh, who inspires me every day; to my extended family, the Jenainatis, for their love and kindness; and Rachel Steel, my son's partner, who brings joy and affection to our family.

While I am immensely thankful to my coaching clients, corporate clients, students and learners, there are too many of them to list here. I do not want to offend by listing some and not others so I will just say that I appreciate my interactions with each one of them. Supporting others to achieve better results and experience greater levels of wellbeing is what makes my work so meaningful.

Finally, I am grateful to my wonderful co-author, David Love. David first introduced me to coaching nearly two decades ago and has been a mentor and wise counsellor ever since. Working with David is always an enriching and positive experience.

## DAVID WRITES

As I start to reflect about the people who have influenced my thinking and approach to reflective practice in professional contexts, I realise the immense number who have been involved. It will prove impossible to include them all here, so I intend to pick out those people who have been the most influential.

I have had the good fortune to work in a number of innovative organisations over the years. I was part of a team that set up a neighbourhood advice centre in London and an array of associated community projects in the 1970s. Making things up as we went along in order to initiate novel ideas, respond to clients and their circumstances, and address the political implications (with a small 'p') of sometimes radical community action involved a great deal of continuous reflective practice – though we did not call it that, or even know such a thing existed. I am immensely grateful to Liz Alderton, Agnes Alexander, Phil Baker, Frances Barnett, Simon Brown, Kaz Burek, Marion East, Dave Ellis, Sara Grossman, Chris Haskett, Colin Langton, Vera Mitchell, Alan Stanton, Marie-Francoise Tollemer and Jonathan and Sushila Zeitlyn.

In the 1980s at Pathway, although in a different field, the team I was part of was adept at coming up with new ways of encouraging debate and action around race equality matters in organisations. Again, I'm not sure we would have recognised the term but looking back now I can see both individual and group reflective practice were key elements of how we approached important challenges. For their insights

I am indebted to Phil Baker, Sheila Cogill, Daphne Crossfield, Denise Gubbay, Zahida Hussain, Amarjit Khera, Helen Marchington, Jane Saunders, Arvind Sharma, Jaswinder Sidhu, Christine Smith and Pete Wilson.

I spent the 1990s in middle and senior management roles in further education, in part contributing to the creation of a new institution out of the merger of four colleges. Once again, although we did not use the terminology, I can see there were facets of reflective practice in how we went about creating a new organisational culture. I owe thanks to Sandra Chalmers, Arvind Sharma and Hilary and Ian Wallis.

In 2000, I joined the Office for Public Management, the UK's first public interest company and an employee-owned development organisation working exclusively with public services. It was here I first encountered the concept of reflective practice both in our work with clients and in our own individual and collective development. With increasing interest in executive coaching, reflective practice became part and parcel of how I approached my work. My thinking and practice were shaped by Sophie Ahmad, Peta Barnes, Ann Bennett, David Bryan, Sheba Cheung, Elaine Clough, Simon Courage, Andrena Cumella, Jude Cummins, Robin Douglas, Anna Eliatamby, Ewan King, Yee-Mai Koo, Hywel Lloyd, Paul Lloyd, Catherine Mangan, Andrew Mann, Clive Miller, Jasmine Miller, Greg Parston, Jonathan Passmore, Ian Roberts, Deborah Rozansky, Sonal Shah, Shannon Shuemake, Paul Tarplett, Carol Ward, Sonia Watson and Sharon Wright.

As a coach, I have a strong commitment to supervision, which embodies reflective practice, and have therefore learnt a great deal about the benefits from the expert supervisors I have worked with over the years, as well as peers in supervision groups. For insightful support and challenge I thank the following supervisors: Jenny Bird, Sarah Goldsworthy, Alison Hodge, Gil Schwenk and Anna Sheather. For engaging in open and honest reflective practice I am extremely grateful to fellow coaches: Bob Baker, Helen Baker, Helen Brown, Lesley Campbell, Stefan Cantore, Sue Goss, Richard Field, Liz Goold, Anita Grabarz, Tamsin Hewitt, Alison Kilduff, Claire Lazarus, Jacqui Moller-Larsen, Munira Thobani, Hilary Samson-Barry, Hilary Thompson, Tim Whitworth and Jude Williams.

In order to teach on the programme, I undertook the Henley Business School Professional Certificate in Coaching, which majors on reflective practice as both a coach development method and a way of being with clients. For stretching my capabilities I am thankful to: Dirk Anthony, Tracy Barr, Julia Carden, Alison Hardingham, Ann James, Jonathan Passmore, Aboodi Shabi and Tatiana Rowson.

In 2023, I was one of the first coaches to take part in the Association for Coaching accredited Diploma in Art-based Coaching, which is designed and led by the artist and coach Anna Sheather of ART in Coaching. Reflective practice and art-based ways of approaching it are central to this programme and I am indebted to Anna, and Sabrina Ahmed and Zita Culkin, my fellow learners, for our many insightful conversations. As part of the coaching practice hours required for this programme, I have had the pleasure of working with a number of impressive coaches, who have therefore contributed directly to my learning about art-based reflective practice. For giving up their time and adding to my understanding of reflective practice I am grateful to: Ana Alexandra Moga, Lynn Dunton, Kara Exner, Anne Lasse, Janina Mainka, Lydia Mastori, Carmen Menea, Daliana Olah and Joanna Williams. In addition, for continually stimulating my interest in creativity in professional settings I am grateful for the work and writings of coaches such as Maxine Bell (art), Jeanette Cowley (art), Claire Bradshaw (nature), Pauline Esson (doodling), Beth Clare McManus (creativity), Anna Sheather (art), Andrea Watts (collaging) and Stephanie Wheeler and Teresa Leyman (playfulness).

Of course, reflecting on my many encounters with clients has also sharpened my reflective practice capabilities – as a coach and supervisor, I learn something from every interaction.

In drawing this consideration of the people who have contributed to my development as reflective professional to a close I want to pay tribute particularly to those people who have each had a profound and enduring impact:

Andrena Cumella (Andrena Cumella Consulting) – for her continuous and unwavering support and constructive challenge through an incalculable number of reflective conversations over so many years.

Anna Eliatamby (clinical psychologist, consultant and coach) – for being the constant source of incisive insights.

Sam Peterson (Sage Therapies & Coaching) – for enabling me to reflect on some very powerful moments from my past and to explore the implications for my thinking, emotions and behaviour in the present.

Anna Sheather (ART in Coaching) – for opening my eyes to the demonstrable power of art in professional settings and for being a role model as a creative reflective practitioner.

Joanna Williams (Flourish) – for expanding my horizons about neurodiversity through our collaborative reflections.

As we emphasise towards the end of this book, reflective practice is not just for work. There is zero doubt that my personal life has benefitted from engaging in reflective practice about matters beyond my professional needs and aspirations. Conversations about politics, humanity, the arts and life in general with those closest to me often involve strong elements of reflection, making the insights all the richer. For that enduring richness I am thankful to friends: John, Barbara and Nancy Bains, Chris Haskett, Julia Holmes, Sue Jarvis, Ian Martin, Vera and Kim Mitchell, David Reading and Rich, Marion, Amy and Peter Seal.

My creative spark, amongst other things, is inspired and nurtured by my close family and I am eternally thankful to Martyn, Julienne, Lauren, Daniel, Beki and Finlay Love, Cic, Bob, Rachel, Phil, Peter and Ann Thorpe, Kathie and David Garfath and David and Judy Brown. In addition, special mention (if only for their toleration of my relentless cartooning about their lives) needs to go to my lifelong partner, Pam, our daughter, Sara, and son, Tom, Ben (Sara's partner) and Bernie (Tom's partner). Without their unconditional love and support none of this would be possible. Last but assuredly not least are my delightful granddaughters, Alba (aged 7) and Rowen (4) whose creativity and playfulness is a true inspiration.

The process of writing this book has been one of continuous reflective practice-in-action as Christian and I have, individually and together, explored in depth what it means to be a reflective practitioner. This has involved working out and road-testing what we think in the first place, grappling with ways to present our ideas cogently and backing out, while all the time learning, from the various cul-de-sacs we have strayed down. For his patience with my highly reflective nature and associated tendency to take my time coming to conclusions, and for his wit and wisdom Christian would have appeared in the list of major influencers of my thinking and practice above – but wielding my power as author I chose to write about him here.

# 1

# THE COMPELLING CASE FOR REFLECTIVE PRACTICE

This chapter will cover:

- The origins of reflective practice
- The benefits of reflective practice
- Current best practice
- An example of Effective Reflective Practice
- Guidance for the reader

Anyone who cares deeply about their personal or professional growth engages in reflective practice. Teachers take time out to reflect on how well a lesson went compared to their original plans. Doctors and health professionals reflect on the quality of their interventions to seek improvements to medical procedures and patient interactions. Artists use 'reflective art statements' to review how they created a piece of art and the intentions behind it. Students reflect on how well they studied for an exam so they can adjust their future revision plans. Human resource managers reflect on how effective their organisation's recruitment processes are at selecting the best candidates. Equality and diversity professionals reflect on the impact they are having on their organisation's practices and procedures so that the prevailing culture promotes inclusion and belonging. Footballers (and their managers) painstakingly take apart what happened in a game so tactics can be improved in the next match. Senior leaders review their leadership styles to ensure they act as role models for others in the organisation. Counsellors and coaches reflect on their interactions with clients to identify how to build and sustain a balance of support and challenge in their working relationships.

Indeed, in many professional fields, reflective practice is an integral part of both the learning and assessment processes associated with initial training and qualification. Reflective practice is seen as an habitual, routine learning activity and as a key means of formally assessing ongoing professional development. For example, in the authors' professional world of executive coaching, reflective practice is a vital means of reviewing and learning from interactions with clients. To gain an initial coaching qualification, coaches are required to *demonstrate* their capacity to reflect on their practice. In addition, trainee coaches learn that reflective practice will become integral to their learning and development throughout their careers. Professional bodies in the field of coaching provide certification of coaches' credentials as their careers progress. The ability to engage in reflective practice is an essential component of the associated assessment process.

Reflective practice is designed to raise self-awareness, which allows us to better understand our own thoughts, emotions, behaviours and actions. The process tends to stimulate our curiosity about how we interact with others and the wider world. Reflection is an essential component of personal growth and enlightenment and a vital feature of many fields of human exploration such as philosophy and psychology. In the work context, self-reflection is the starting point for the learning that underpins improved performance.

## THE ORIGINS OF REFLECTIVE PRACTICE

What is reflective practice? American educator and psychologist John Dewey defined reflective practice as 'the active, persistent and careful consideration of any belief or supposed form of knowledge in the light of the grounds that support it' (1910, p. 6). Reflective practice involves 'a conversation with the situation' that 'enables us to direct our actions with foresight ... it enables us to know what we are about when we act' (1910, p. 6). This perspective alerts us to the importance of considering the values and beliefs that inform our actions and not just the functional aspects of what we did and how it landed. Another influential writer, Donald Schön, built on Dewey's ideas by defining reflective practice as an ability to reflect on one's actions as part of a process of continual learning (2016).

In his seminal work *The Reflective Practitioner*, Schön criticises purely scientific, rational approaches to solving problems. He argues that such an approach ignores the reality of what professionals actually do. According to Schön, people are not always capable of describing their actions accurately even though they know more than they are able to verbalise. This level of knowledge in Schön's thinking, falls into the 'knowing how' category. This contrasts with the 'knowing what' category, which is more scientific and rational and therefore easier to describe. Schön places high value on the insights that arise from experience and direct involvement with the situation and the context of the professional. In addition, he asserts that our knowledge, at least in part, arises from our actions.

By exploring the relationship between knowledge and action, professionals can gain insights into their thought processes. Thus by focusing on the reality of their experience, the professional is enabled to make more of their 'knowing how' knowledge available for scrutiny. This allows them to explore the thinking that underpins it. Schön believes that professionals strengthen their competence as much through reflecting on experience as through gaining knowledge from books or learning programmes. He sees reflective learning as a continuous cycle, rather than a linear or functional process.

According to Schön, reflective practice is the means by which professionals become aware of their implicit, and partially hidden, knowledge. It is how they learn from experience. Two kinds of reflective practice are identified:

- reflection-on-action, which takes place after the event and requires time for a more considered review
- reflection-in-action, which involves in-the-moment reflection in order to adjust our behaviour to meet the changing circumstances in front of us.

While Schön has undoubtedly made a major contribution to thinking and practice about reflection, his assertions have encountered some criticism. Firstly, his conclusions take little account of the difficulties associated with the practicalities of creating space and time in busy professional lives to do the required work. Secondly, reflection-in-action is easier said than done for most people, given how difficult it can be for a professional to distance themselves from the lived experience in the moment. Finally, a strong case can be made for an additional form of reflection, reflection-*before*-action where the same rigour and focus on a future, anticipated reality can produce beneficial learning (Edwards, 2017).

## THE BENEFITS OF REFLECTIVE PRACTICE

It is widely accepted that reflective practice has important benefits. These include gaining new knowledge and the modification of existing knowledge as well as an improved understanding of the connections between theory and practice. Reflective practice can lead to an improved understanding of the rationale behind a professional's actions and behaviours, and of their personal decision-making criteria. Professionals can also achieve greater awareness of how their assumptions, values and beliefs impact their own thinking, feelings and behaviour. Insights can also include a deeper and more grounded self-awareness, including increased clarity about a professional's strengths and areas for development. The habit of reflective practice can produce enhanced analytical and evaluative capabilities and an increased sense of autonomy, competence and control. Finally, professionals can gain greater confidence and motivation to take actions that lead to improvements in their performance.

## CURRENT BEST PRACTICE

Many writers have proposed valuable ways of engaging in reflective practice. Here we will briefly outline four frameworks that professionals commonly use:

### Gibbs' Reflective Cycle

Graham Gibbs (1988) offers a series of stages for reflective practice. The first stage, *description*, involves outlining what happened in a situation without analysis or judgement and focusing on the facts of the situation. The *feelings* stage encourages an exploration of the emotions the professional felt at the time, and later with hindsight. Again, analysis and judgement are avoided. The third part of the cycle focuses on *evaluation*, where the professional identifies what went well, and not so well. This is followed by *analysis*, in which the professional attempts to make sense of everything that happened and find possible drivers for what worked well and less well. Based on this analysis, the professional then draws out *conclusions*. The cycle encourages general conclusions as the starting point, followed by conclusions that are specific to the situation. The final *action plan* stage involves deciding the practical implications of those conclusions and the actions that need to be put in place.

### Kolb's Reflective Cycle

David Kolb identified four ways in which people learn based on an experiential learning theory (1984). In Kolb's thinking, new learning arises out of novel experiences: 'Learning is the process whereby knowledge is created through the transformation of experience' (Kolb, 1984, p. 38). Central to Kolb's theory is the notion that the professional must engage with all four parts of the cycle for the benefits of the learning to be fully realised.

Kolb's learning cycle can be entered at any of the four points. Used as a reflective framework, the starting point is most typically *concrete experience*, which centres on what actually happened. The professional focuses on that experience in the next stage of the cycle: *reflective observation*. Here, the professional reflects on their experience in the light of their existing knowledge. They are encouraged to identify similarities and inconsistencies between their experience and understanding. From their reflections, the professional creates a new idea or theory about the situation they are exploring or modifies their existing thinking to better match the circumstances. In this *abstract conceptualisation* stage, the professional is learning from experience and linking this to, or amending, their theoretical understanding. This new or modified idea is tested through *active experimentation* where the professional applies their new learning in the real world and thereby revisits the *concrete experience* part of the cycle. In Figure 1.1, we have combined the Gibbs and Kolb cycles to create one coherent process of reflection. The figure-of-eight introduces

Kolb's learning phases into Gibbs' 'Making Sense' stage bringing the insights from a more detailed consideration of the different sources of learning into play.

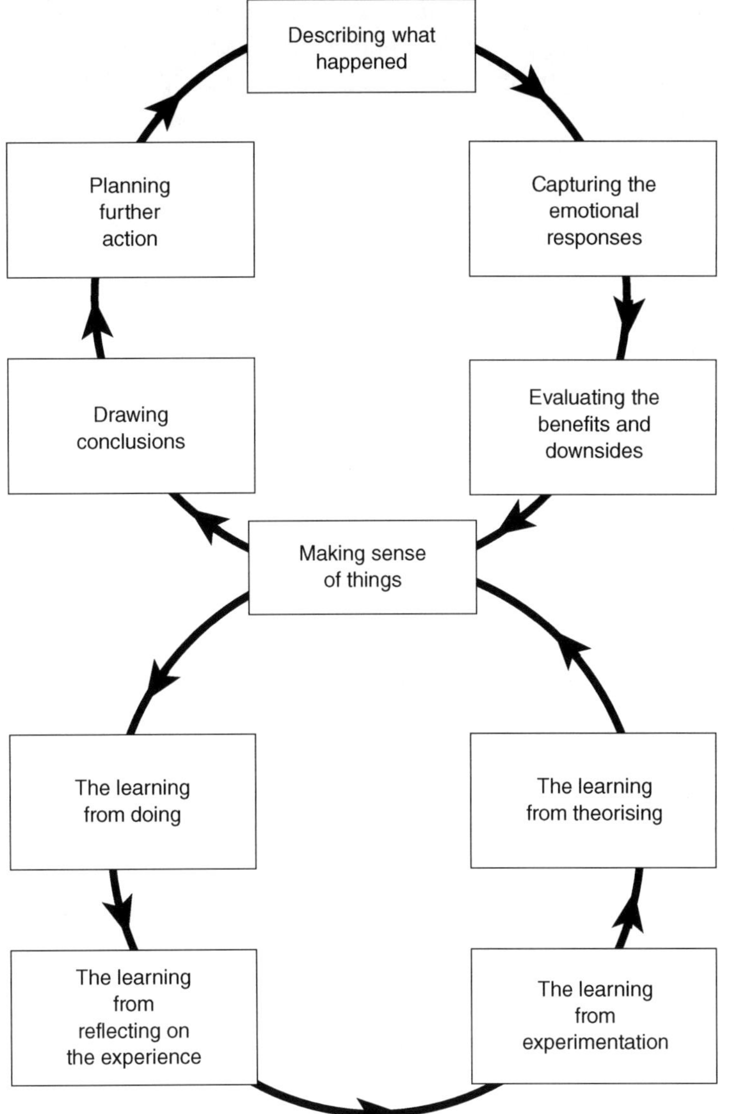


**Figure 1.1** Gibbs and Kolb cycles combined

Kolb's learning cycle (1984) gives rise to four associated learning styles, which were subsequently devised by Peter Honey and Alan Mumford (1986): Activist, Reflector, Theorist and Pragmatist. In Chapter 6 we explore in more detail the implications of these learning styles, and other learning preferences for Effective Reflective Practice.

## Moon's Approach to Reflective Writing

Jenny Moon (1999) positions reflective writing as capturing the outputs of the thinking that takes place during reflection. She recognises other possible media for capturing reflections such as drawing, photography, video and music. According to Moon, we shape our reflections based on influences such as the purpose of the writing; whether it is for private or public consumption; our emotional response to the event being written about and the act of writing about it; and our skill in reflective writing.

Moon suggests there are four levels of reflective writing, with the last exhibiting the greatest depth and breadth of focus. The first level involves describing what happened, focusing on the facts of a situation with little or no analysis of the implications. At the second level, the reflective writing is superficial, making reference only to the bare facts. The third level of reflective writing shows a degree of self-awareness and acknowledges intentions and motivations, and their impact. In the fourth level, the professional demonstrates an objective overview of what happened, shows curiosity about what they are noticing and identifies insights and learning they will put into practice.

## The Henley 8 Reflective Framework

Building on Moon's approach to reflective writing, Jonathan Passmore and Tracy Sinclair developed the Henley 8 Reflective Framework for Coaches (cited in James in Passmore (ed.) 2021). The framework consists of eight focused questions to guide exploration while maintaining a focus on the professional's assumptions, values and beliefs. The framework is adapted below for wider application:

1 What did I *observe?* (noting visual and auditory evidence that could be picked up by a video camera)
2 What was *my response?* (noting emotions, physical sensations or physiological indicators evoked by what just happened)
3 What does this tell me *about me?* (rather than what does this tell me about others)
4 What does this tell me about myself *as a professional?* (based on what I have just learnt about myself)
5 What *strengths* does this offer? (how what I have just learnt about myself might serve my practice)
6 What are the potential *pitfalls?* (how what I have just learnt about myself might hinder my practice)
7 What did I *learn?* (noting what I can take forward in my practice)
8 What will I *do differently* next time? (committing to applying the learning).

# A WORKED EXAMPLE OF REFLECTIVE PRACTICE AND WRITING

Now that we have surveyed some popular reflective practice frameworks, it may be helpful to consider how they can be used in real world situations. We will explore an example of reflective practice which illustrates Schön's reflection-on-action and reflection-in-action. Below is one of the authors reflecting on a coaching conversation with a client and exploring the implications for their practice. In this example, the author has used the Henley 8 Reflective Framework as a starting point.

## Reflecting on Practice

### Drawn Towards a Vortex of Negativity

I noticed a growing morbid fascination with the negative aspects of my client's situation and that I was being drawn into the complexities of their experience. It reminded me of conversations I have had with someone close to me in the midst of one of their severe bouts of depression - a sense of being caught up in a vortex of negativity. The client was looking to me for approval of the statements they were making as if to gain confirmation that their overall negative demeanour was appropriate in the circumstances.

There were moments when I got a fly-on-the-wall perspective on the conversation and I became intrigued by wondering how I could enable my client to achieve anything like a positive outcome given their doom-laden starting point. I felt frustrated as my attempts to find any positives in the situation continued to fail. The client did come up with some positive ideas but they would soon find the in-built negative connotations as they perceived them.

It was clear that my usual positive approach to coaching conversations was unlikely to work on this occasion. Aside from my client's determination to view everything negatively, this would come across as patronising or could easily be received as a thinly veiled admonition to 'buck up'. It felt important not to collude with the client's negative perspective and I was concerned not to get pulled into 'rabbit holes'.

This conversation posed a challenge to my usual positivity. I was intrigued that, despite my frustrations, I was comfortable with my client's 'gloomy' outlook and despondency that seemed to be associated with their worldview. Given my strong preference for maintaining control over the overall structure of the conversation, I might have expected to be even more discomfited especially as the client was struggling to establish clear expectations for the conversation.

*(Continued)*

Earlier in my career as a coach, I would have struggled – not knowing how to turn the conversation into something constructive. I realised I was feeling OK with the negativity and was able to use this to enable the client to explore their negative perceptions. I felt confident that delving into 'the gloom' would ultimately prove fruitful.

I felt the client was attempting to shock me. I also sensed that perhaps I was the first person to take 'the gloom' seriously and allow the client to delve into it purposely. I was surprised to notice that I didn't feel shocked, and I stuck with my approach until the client started to have insights.

Feedback from colleagues over the years suggests that I am a good listener. I think this ability drew me to coaching in the first place. My reflections about this interaction have indicated some important personal strengths. For example, I noticed that I can be tenacious in challenging situations. I can get concerned about the anticipation of a challenge but when faced with it, am calm and purposeful in the moment.

There were times in this conversation where I was not sure what I was going to do next. However, on each occasion ideas came to me and when I pursued them progress was made. This suggests I can be inventive 'on the spot' and that I should trust in this ability to make things happen. I know I have a very strong preference to want to build rapport with clients, to enthuse them and to structure conversations so that they are productive. Throughout the conversation I remained acutely focused on the client, which will have communicated that I cared about their wellbeing.

My reflections have also highlighted some potential problematic areas. Early in this conversation I felt too drawn into my fascination with the negativity, which might have compromised my independent perspective and undermined the ideas that emerged later about where to take the conversation. My tendency to focus on the emotional elements at play can be very helpful at times but can mean I might become more personally involved with clients and their issues. I need to be careful this does not cause me to hold back from making challenging interventions that stretch the client. In intentionally focusing on the negative elements of the situation there is a danger I reinforce the client's despondency. Delving into darker territory without a positive outcome could be potentially damaging for the client.

So, what learning do I take from all this? I need to notice, then set aside, when a conversation triggers an emotional connection for me. In addition, I should place more faith in my ability to find ways that engage clients, even when they are expressing negative perceptions. It is important for clients to feel they are being truly heard. Acknowledging their perceptions, before challenging them provides a strong basis for potential insights.

This experience re-affirmed my belief that a visual approach can be very effective. We mapped the negatives using sticky notes and the resulting bleak picture increased the client's commitment to making a positive change. There were several critical moments in this conversation and working with them led to positive progress for the client. This experience reinforces my belief that the relationship is at the heart of coaching effectiveness. I need to notice when this focus on sustaining the relationship might override the identification of practical actions. As a coach with a strong reflector learning style, I can have a tendency to prioritise insight over concrete action.

In this example, we can see the essential elements of reflective practice in play. Both of Schön's dimensions are illustrated: clearly most of the reflection happens with hindsight after the event (reflection-on-action). However, there are also clear instances of reflection-in-action where shifts in approach have resulted from in-the-moment evaluation. In addition, the reflections focus on how the professional felt about what was happening. The important emotional factors which are driving the professional's thinking and actions are at the forefront, producing a richer picture than a straightforward factual account of the conversation. It is also interesting that the professional includes very little about their client's situation, choosing to focus entirely on the impacts of the experience on themselves. Towards the end of the account, the professional draws out strengths and potential pitfalls identified as a result of the reflective process and begins to identify implications for their practice.

This example also highlights a concern for the wellbeing of the client, and tangentially, the wellbeing of the professional. We firmly believe that a focus on wellbeing, of both client and professional, is an essential component of what we, the authors, believe is Effective Reflective Practice. Positive psychology places great importance on wellbeing as a crucial outcome of all human endeavours. In addition, the authors both supervise coach practice and enabling coaches to engage in reflection-on-action is a foundational part of our work. Good practice in supervision includes a restorative element (Proctor, 2008) to support coaches' overall wellbeing by exploring factors in the coaching relationship which have had an impact on the coach and need acknowledgement or release. That impact may be minor but may still be revealed in supervision to be important to reflect upon in order to unearth the insights for improved practice. On the other hand, the impact on the coach may be major causing anxiety or even trauma and the coach needs time, space and support in achieving catharsis as a precursor to incorporating the learning into their practice.

So far, we have seen that reflective practice includes an exploration of a professional's personal experience of their work, which moves beyond a functional focus on what went well, or not so well, and the learning that arises as a result. Effective Reflective Practice also includes consideration of the emotions generated by the experience as well as the assumptions, values and beliefs that underpin the professional's behaviour and actions. Effective Reflective Practice is much more than an introspective, navel-gazing activity. It leads to insights and learning which are then translated into purposeful action. Reflective practice is an ongoing process, which continually reviews thoughts, feelings and actions. In this book, we are proposing that Effective Reflective Practice will lead to greater self-awareness, improvements in practice and stronger relationships with clients and colleagues.

We strongly believe that the most powerful and influential reflective practice will only occur when account is taken of the context in which professionals are working. We propose that a systemic approach is needed so that the external factors impacting professionals and their clients can be explored.

The pressures experienced by people and professions as a result of the major challenges confronting the world such as the Covid-19 pandemic and its aftermath, personal and global economic challenges, continuing wars and the climate crisis further underline the importance of adopting a systemic perspective and emphasising the importance of wellbeing. Approaches to reflective practice that do not include these two elements will not serve humanity in these extremely challenging times.

> 'We are inclined to think of reflection as something quiet and personal. My argument ... is that reflection is action-oriented, social and political. Its 'product' is praxis (informed, committed action), the most eloquent and socially significant form of human action'. (Kemmis, 1985, p. 139)

Bringing all these features together there is another overarching element we wish to add to the thinking about reflective practice that makes the process even more powerful. This element is alignment. For positive, sustainable outcomes to be achieved the following need to be aligned:

- internal factors, including the alignment of personal values and beliefs with wellbeing
- external factors, including the alignment of personal insights and learning with the desired outcomes of the reflective process
- contextual and cultural factors, including the alignment of individuals' behaviours with systemic forces, or with strategies for eliminating or mitigating the negative impacts of those forces.

## Summary: Effective Reflective Practice

Effective Reflective Practice involves:

- evaluating personal experience
- exploring assumptions, values and beliefs

- generating insights and learning
- actioning the insights and learning in the service of clients
- reviewing the effectiveness of the changed behaviours
- paying attention to the wellbeing of everyone involved
- taking full account of the systemic factors that impact professionals and their clients
- noticing the degrees of alignment between the essential factors.

In this book, we build on and extend the best practice ideas we have described in this chapter to create a new framework that meets the requirements of our times and provides a sound foundation for engaging in Effective Reflective Practice.

## YOU, OUR READER

We see at least three audiences for this book. The first are those readers who want to be good reflective practitioners. This group of readers will be asking the question 'How can I enhance my ability to undertake Effective Reflective Practice?' The second are those professionals who want to use reflective writing as an integral part of their reflection process. This group of readers will be asking the question 'How do I use writing as a means of reflecting on my practice?' The third involves readers going through an accreditation process to achieve an academic or vocational qualification in a particular field. This may include certification of their practice with a professional body. The demands of the assessment process will almost certainly involve demonstrating an ability to reflect on their practice through the submission of written reflective pieces. This group of readers will be asking the question 'How do I provide written evidence of Effective Reflective Practice?' If you fall into any of these categories, this book has been designed for you.

To write effective reflective notes or assignments the writer needs to have a full understanding of all the components of Effective Reflective Practice. Otherwise, there is a risk that the process becomes a functional exercise for meeting assessment requirements rather than a genuine act of purposeful self-reflection focused on outcomes for personal and professional improvement. By engaging fully with the process, professionals will develop an ingrained and sustainable habit of reflection that will serve them well as their careers develop. Professionals who care deeply about their work need to commit to creating the space for reflective practice.

> It's hard to look at modern life and see our capacities for reflection or meaning-making. We don't use our gifts to be more aware or thoughtful. We're driven in the opposite direction. Things move too fast for us to

> reflect, demanding tasks give us no time to think, and we barely notice the lack of meaning until forced to stand still by illness, tragedy, or job loss. But in spite of our hurry, we cannot stop life's dynamic of self-reference or the human need for meaning. If we want to influence any change, anywhere, we need to work *with* this powerful process rather than deny its existence. (Wheatley, 2006, p. 147)

In this chapter we have outlined the benefits of Effective Reflective Practice so that professionals can continually enhance their capacity to serve clients and stakeholders to the highest standards. In addition, making Effective Reflective Practice a habit is one way of taking time out from the increasingly intense bustle of our working lives. We need time to breathe and reflect. Professional bodies, universities, colleges and training organisations place reflective practice at the heart of initial and continuous development because they believe in its capacity to generate insights and lifelong learning.

There are risks of *not* building reflective practice into our professional lives. If we do not take time to reflect, we are missing out on a wealth of information about ourselves as professionals and human beings. We fail to learn from our mistakes, 'near-misses' and successes. There is also a danger we become complacent about the quality of our contribution to the world. We risk not living up to the professional standards expected of us.

There is a moral imperative on us to always be striving to strengthen our practice in the service of our clients. We should engage with reflective practice with humility, honesty and self-compassion so that we have as accurate and balanced a view of our effectiveness and impact on others as possible. More widely, reflective practice is a foundation stone for the creative work that needs to be undertaken to overcome the significant challenges facing humanity. In this book, you are invited to work towards achieving a way of being that supports your professional practice and allows you to be at your best. Reflective practice which is built on the realities of your working relationships with clients will stretch your capabilities as a professional.

## HOW TO ENGAGE WITH THIS BOOK

We intend this to be a practical guide to reflective practice and reflective writing. We have followed a clear structure:

- an introduction to reflective practice
- a presentation of the principles that inform Effective Reflective Practice
- a step-by-step description of a new framework
- an explanation of how to demonstrate reflective practice through writing
- an exploration of how to deploy creativity when engaging in reflective practice
- a discussion about how to create environments that encourage reflective practice
- an invitation to make Effective Reflective Practice a habit.

On an accompanying website you will find resources from the book which will support your reflective practice including, for example, templates for your planning and colour versions of the figures we include in these pages. You will find a list of these additional resources on p. vii.

As you will have seen from our biographies earlier in this book, we, the authors, are both executive coaches and coach supervisors. Between us we also have extensive experience of organisational, leadership and teacher development. Given reflective practice is one key component of effective coaching and supervision we draw heavily on these areas of expertise and experience. Alongside other sources you will find a number of coaching-related books and resources in our 'Find Out More' sections at the end of each chapter and in the list of references at the end of the book. If you are not a coach, it is possible you will not be keen to delve into these resources. However, there is much rich thinking and practice in these materials that are applicable to Effective Reflective Practice. We have therefore included suggested websites to visit. While some of these will inevitably be coaching focused they will give you access to a range of ideas and resources that are eminently adaptable for use in your reflective practice.

We would like you to be active participants as you read, so we have included practical activities for you to undertake as you progress through the book. Here is your first activity:

## Putting it into Practice

### Getting Started

Get yourself a journal - one you can write, sketch and doodle in - and one that inspires you to make notes. This journal will be your own private and personal record of your reflections as you work through the book - where anything goes. Be as creative as you would like when capturing your reflections. Do this in ways that you are comfortable with *and* step outside your comfort zones to experiment with new ways of doing things.

Focusing on the Kolb learning cycle and Honey and Mumford's learning styles (for more detail see Chapter 6):

- What is your preferred learning style? You are likely to have a preference for more than one style. Remember that Kolb (1984) asserts that the best learning occurs when all four parts of the cycle are in play. How might you bring all four styles into your learning journey?
- How might your preferences help or hinder your capacity to reflect? How might you strengthen those factors that help while minimising those that hinder?

*(Continued)*

- Peter Honey and Alan Mumford have devised a Learning Style Inventory based on Kolb's learning cycle. You can complete a free questionnaire online to find out more about your learning preferences. Look for 'Honey & Mumford Learning Style Questionnaire' online. As with all such questionnaires they provide you with data to consider and accept or reject. Do the results chime with your own thoughts about your preferred style(s)? It can be helpful to check with trusted relatives, friends and colleagues how they see your preferences. Again, these are data for you to add into the conversation with yourself.

## SUMMARY

In this chapter we have explained why we believe reflective practice is essential for personal and professional development. We have outlined the ideas of some key thinkers in the fields of reflective practice and of learning. We provided an example of a piece of reflective writing which emphasised that capturing the learning from reflection is much more than simply outlining 'the facts'. Finally, we are encouraging you to make a start on your reflective journey by beginning to journal about your professional activities and relationships with clients.

### Find Out More

Edwards, S. (2017). Reflecting differently. New dimensions: Reflection-before-action and reflection-beyond-action. *International Practice Development Journal* 7: 1-14.

Gibbs, G. (1988). *Learning by Doing: A Guide to Teaching and Learning Methods.* Further Education Unit. Oxford: Oxford Polytechnic.

Honey, P. & Mumford, A. (1986). *Learning Styles Questionnaire.* London: Peter Honey Publications.

Moon, J. (1999). *Reflection in Learning and Professional Development.* London: Kogan Page.

Schön, D. (2016). *The Reflective Practitioner: How Professionals Think in Action.* Abingdon: Routledge.

# 2

# FOUNDATIONAL PRINCIPLES AND PURPOSES

This chapter will cover:

- The foundational principles of Effective Reflective Practice
    - Awareness
    - Openness
    - Intentionality
    - Compassion
- The purposes of Effective Reflective Practice
    - Learning
    - Change
    - Alignment
    - Presence

We have already set out why Effective Reflective Practice has become critically important during our times. We acknowledged the growing interest in reflective practice across a wide range of professional contexts and then considered existing best practice in the field. In this chapter, we propose a new approach to reflective practice that meets the evolving needs of professionals. The purpose of this book is to present, clearly and explicitly, an approach to reflective practice that is implementable, impactful and demonstrable. By working through this book, chapter by chapter, you will deepen your understanding of reflective practice, learn the skills you need to practise until it becomes a habit, and be able to demonstrate how your use of reflective practice leads to personal and professional learning and growth.

The approach to reflective practice that we will be presenting in this book goes beyond the simple aim of professional improvement. In fact, we will be sharing *four* purposes of reflective practice. These will be presented later in the chapter. Before we turn our attention to the purposes, we would like to establish some *foundational principles* of reflective practice. They are *awareness*, *openness*, *intentionality* and *compassion* (see Figure 2.1). People wishing to undertake Effective Reflective Practice should consider and adopt these principles.

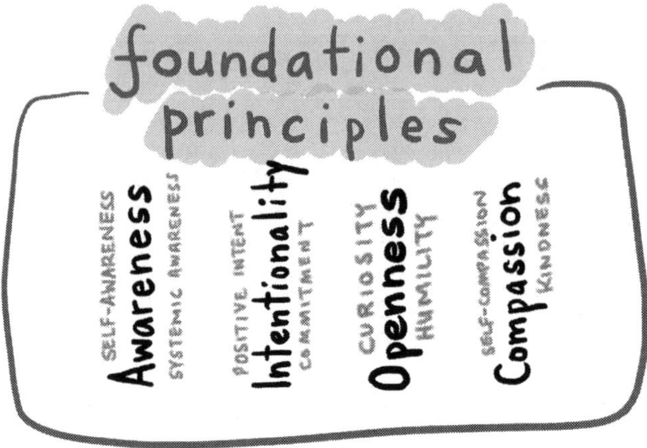


**Figure 2.1** Foundational principles of Effective Reflective Practice

## FOUNDATIONAL PRINCIPLES OF EFFECTIVE REFLECTIVE PRACTICE

### Awareness

There can be no learning or self-development without a fundamental sense of awareness (of one's self and of one's environment). Such awareness, even if it is at a basic level, is a prerequisite for any reflective practice. Two types of awareness are relevant for reflective practitioners, self-awareness and systemic awareness. Both are of value and importance.

#### Self-Awareness

Self-awareness is the ability to understand how one thinks, feels and behaves. Without this understanding, there is no basis for self-reflection. For example, if a person has little self-awareness, they will not be able to understand why they behave the way they do or predict how they will react in various situations. Conversely, people who are self-aware can tell when they are happy, they can sense when they are starting to feel nervous, they can identify their strengths and areas for development and are better able to predict how they will behave in a variety of circumstances. Self-awareness can be summarised as a good understanding of oneself. The reason that this is fundamental for reflective practice is because a person cannot effectively plan to make improvements or changes to their life if they do not have an understanding of how they are at the moment. A good level of self-awareness means that a person has a clear sense of their starting point in relation to any improvements or enhancements that they may be working towards.

### Systemic Awareness

Systemic awareness is an understanding of how we operate within our personal, societal and professional contexts. Having this awareness means that people understand how they interact with others and the environment. It is based on the view that organisations, societies and other groups are always changing, organic and interconnected. Systems theory is a field of study that investigates how systems relate and interact with one another and argues that individual components of a system cannot be understood or explained simply. To make changes, it is necessary to acknowledge the complexity of systems and relationships.

## Openness

Effective Reflective Practice, and indeed learning of any kind, requires openness to ideas and new insights. The reflective practitioner will derive more out of the process if they are open-minded – open to feedback, open to trying new things and generally receptive to information or insights generated through the reflective practice process. There are two aspects of openness that are particularly relevant: curiosity and humility.

### Curiosity

Curiosity is an attitude of inquisitiveness that makes us want to know more about something. In this case, this curiosity should be directed to ourselves, how we behave in the world, our relationships and the impact that we are having. Curiosity is an important aspect of openness because it urges us to be open to new ideas and to see things with fresh eyes. Humility is another aspect of openness.

### Humility

Humility is the quality of being modest. Reflective practitioners should not overestimate their knowledge, skills, importance or abilities. Humility can be described as an openness to *not* knowing. By acknowledging what we do not know, it becomes easier to reflect on what we *do* know and what we have achieved. As a result, we are better learners when we are humble. Humility rescues us from the conviction of being right and releases us from holding 'truths' to be sacrosanct. By adopting openness (humility and curiosity), we are more likely to benefit from the process of Effective Reflective Practice.

## Intentionality

Above all else, reflective practice is *intentional* practice. In other words, reflective practice begins with an intention to enhance one's practice in one way or another. Clarifying the intention before the start of a reflective practice process (the Effective Reflective Practice framework will be presented in Chapter 3) increases the chances of positive outcomes. Traditionally, reflective practice has focused narrowly on improving one's professional practice. That is certainly one intention. However, later in this chapter, we propose that we may benefit from broadening our perspective to include other powerful intentions. Two aspects of intentionality are important to consider – positive intent and commitment.

### Positive Intent

Underpinning successful reflective practice is a clearly-defined positive intent. Those undertaking Effective Reflective Practice should consider and make explicit their positive intention. As examples, a health professional may be seeking to improve their 'bedside manner' to provide more compassionate support for their patients; a senior leader may be working to improve their interactions with their team members to be more inspiring and encouraging; an executive coach may be interested in enhancing their rapport-building ability so that their clients feel at ease more quickly. Articulating these positive intentions is critical to Effective Reflective Practice as we will discuss later in this chapter.

### Commitment

Alongside positive intention, Effective Reflective Practice requires the commitment necessary to see it through. Change and learning are not always easy, so it is likely that resilience and tenacity will be needed. A high level of commitment ensures that the desired changes are achieved. Establishing one's commitment and regularly checking in on motivation and energy levels will enhance a person's ability to undertake Effective Reflective Practice.

## Compassion

Compassion is described as the ability to show empathy and concern for misfortunes. This element is sometimes overlooked, leading to risks to implementation of changes. Lack of compassion can have a negative impact on a person's wellbeing. Often, the assumption is that compassion relates to the suffering of *others*. Since Effective Reflective Practice requires self-awareness and openness to receiving feedback, it becomes imperative for the desired results and the person's wellbeing that reflective practitioners show compassion to themselves as well as others.

## Self-Compassion

Effective Reflective Practice requires exploring one's strengths and areas for development. It is likely that people will need to examine their mistakes and errors of judgement alongside their skills and moments of brilliance. Self-compassion will be needed to ensure that people do not become overly self-critical, chastising themselves for their flaws. With kindness and care towards themselves, it is easier for people to acknowledge weaknesses without impacting negatively on their self-esteem, motivation or energy levels. Those who take a compassionate approach to reflective practice ensure that their self-talk does not become overly negative. This protects their positive self-regard and sense of worth as they learn more and work to improve. Even better, when the desired changes are achieved, this will boost wellbeing and self-esteem.

## Kindness

While reflective practice tends to focus on learning about how professionals can enhance their own performance in some way, it is most effective when they take time to consider their contexts and important relationships. In other words, assessing their relationships with other people is a necessary part of the reflective process. When considering how other people are affecting their practice, it is beneficial to be kind and compassionate. This is so that other people and important relationships can be assessed fairly, giving others the benefit of the doubt and remaining open to multiple perspectives and explanations.

In the section above, we have set out the foundational principles of Effective Reflective Practice. Adopting these principles will enhance your ability to undertake Effective Reflective Practice, allowing you to become the kind of professional that you aspire to being. Taking these principles to heart is the first step on your learning journey.

### Getting Started

We have referred to these as foundational principles because they form the basis of Effective Reflective Practice. Take some time to consider each of the four principles. Create a page of notes for each of the foundational principles and jot down your initial reactions to each of the elements.

- What is your immediate response?
- How do you feel as you consider adopting these principles?

*(Continued)*

- To what extent are you drawn to certain principles?
- To what extent are you resistant to some of them?

Capture your notes in your learning journal so that you can return to them periodically as you work through this book.

## THE FOUR PURPOSES OF REFLECTIVE PRACTICE

Now, let us turn our attention to the purposes of Effective Reflective Practice (see Figure 2.2). The most obvious ones are to *learn* and to bring about *change*. In fact, it could be argued that if learning does not take place or change does not occur, then reflective practice has not been successful. This is a convincing argument, but Effective Reflective Practice promises much more than learning and change. It can be harnessed to increase *alignment* too. And beyond the benefits to professional practice, those who undertake Effective Reflective Practice can enhance the quality of their *presence*, experiencing everyday interactions more positively.

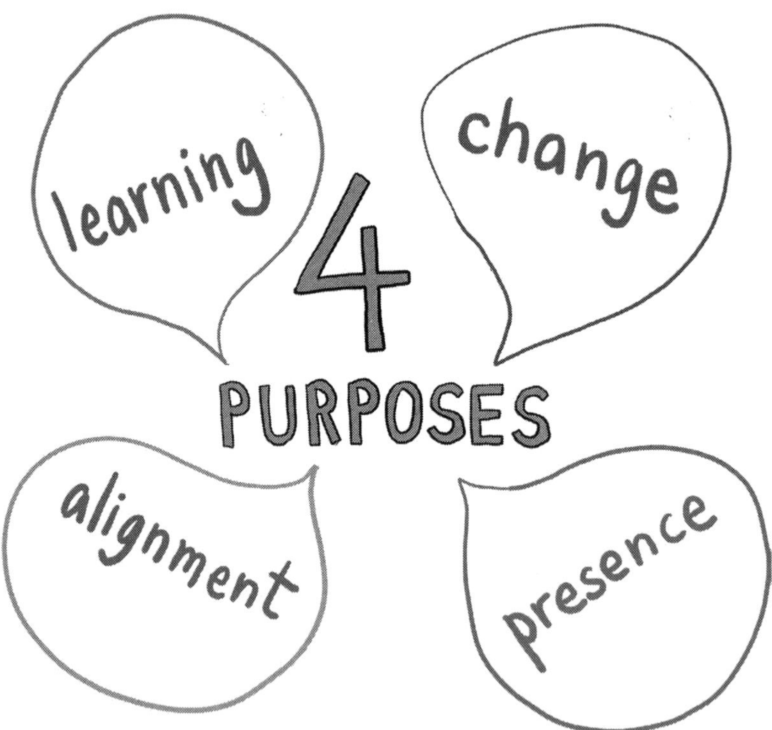


**Figure 2.2** The four purposes of reflective practice

We will consider the four purposes below, starting with the two most-often quoted reasons for undertaking reflective practice.

## Learning

Reflective practice is often classified as a learning methodology. Some would argue that its primary function is to support 'on-the-job' learning. By bringing intentional attention to people's professional practice, the process of reflective practice supports them to learn how to improve in certain professional contexts. The learning generated from this process is then deployed to develop theories about how people might perform differently. In this way, the learning is used immediately, and people can then experiment with new behaviours or practices. This, of course, leads to new learning, and the cycle continues. Essentially, reflective practice is a cycle of ongoing learning.

It is important for us to set aside some time at this point to reflect on *what* people learn through reflective practice. The good news is that there are so many things that can be learnt through the process (see Table 2.1). First, people learn about what is working in their professional practice. Second, they learn what can be improved. Third, people can learn about their likes or dislikes. Fourth, people can learn about their feelings. Fifth, how thoughts can enhance or diminish their performance. Sixth, how they perform differently depending on the context. Seventh, how their relationships help or hinder their performance. This is only a partial list – there is so much learning to be gained! In Effective Reflective Practice, the fundamental question is 'what do I need to learn to be even better at what I do?' For each person, that answer will be different.

**Table 2.1** What can be learnt through reflective practice

| |
|---|
| What is already working? |
| What can be improved? |
| What are my likes and dislikes? |
| What emotions are involved? |
| How should I think about this? |
| How is the context affecting me? |
| How am I relating with others? |

## Change

Another reason there is so much interest in reflective practice is that it is also a process for bringing about change. It could be argued that learning alone is of little use if it does not lead to a change in professional practice. In fact, the two (learning and change) are intertwined, because simply changing behaviours without careful consideration is unlikely to bring about sustainable improvements. Effective Reflective Practice is the opposite of a random 'try it and see what happens' type of approach. It is deliberate and informed by relevant on-the-job learning. Effective Reflective Practice can drive continuous improvement by allowing people to regularly evaluate how they are doing, leading to a virtuous cycle of greater learning, better performance and increased curiosity. Individual reflective practice can also impact wider change in organisations and systems, especially if there are processes in place for sharing the outcomes and exploring their implications for collective action.

If reflective practice is a change methodology, as we are proposing, then it is useful to consider how it relates to a leading theory of change. Intentional change theory (Boyatzis, 2006) posits that change is more likely to take place when there is a compelling goal. In other words, people undertaking reflective practice should be drawn towards a desired future state that is meaningful to them. Goal theory (Locke & Latham, 2002) would suggest that a person's goals should be self-identified, desired and compelling. Once the goal is clear, the person making the change should work towards a better understanding of where they are at present, in relation to that goal. This means that information or data need to be gathered – a central feature of reflective practice. Such information will be more useful if it takes place in the person's professional context and is collected by the person wishing to make the change. Once the person has a compelling goal and is clear where they are in relation to that goal, then it becomes important for them to come up with ideas about how to move towards the goal. Once ideas have been generated, the person can start experimenting to identify a strategy that is helpful in supporting them to make progress towards their goal. Intentional change theory also highlights the importance of social support in making change happen. This is addressed in Effective Reflective Practice by bringing relationships into the frame of the learning project. Some forms of reflective practice include social support, either by working in pairs or small groups (this will be discussed further in Chapter 8). In summary, since Effective Reflective Practice aims to bring about change, it is important to have a clear and compelling goal. Having a clear sense of a desirable future will motivate us, make us braver, increase our commitment and support us to weather challenges.

## What is your Compelling Goal?

Take some time to identify a professional goal that is genuinely compelling and engaging.

Write down the goal and then capture some notes in your learning journal about what motivates you to achieve it.

## Alignment

Even though the benefits of using reflective practice to enhance alignment might be the most significant, this purpose is often overlooked. The process of considered, intentional reflective practice provides an ideal opportunity for people to ensure alignment in many aspects of their lives. First, professionals can assess whether their everyday behaviours and interactions are aligned to their values. For example, a person who values honesty and authenticity, but works in a job that requires them to aggressively sell insurance policies to people who will not benefit from them, might find that their behaviours are not aligned to their values. The situation is not good for the professional's clients, and it can be stressful having to continually behave in ways that are not aligned to one's values. Second, misalignment can occur when a person realises that they say one thing, but then do something different. What is said and what is done can be brought into greater alignment through Effective Reflective Practice. Third, people can review how aligned they are with people around them. This can include friends, family, colleagues and members of a community. If there is misalignment in these important relationships, this can cause stress and have a negative impact on wellbeing. Fourth, alignment between a person and their worldview or faith leads to a positive sense of meaning and purpose.

Take some notes in your learning journal. Rate yourself as 'highly aligned', 'aligned', 'slightly aligned' or 'not aligned' on the following:

- Everyday interactions and behaviours with deeply-held personal values
- What you say and what you actually do
- Important personal relationships
- Important professional relationships
- What is meaningful for you (worldview or faith).

Which area of alignment is most important to you at the moment?

## Presence (in the Moment)

This is perhaps the least-mentioned purpose of reflective practice. Learning about oneself and others; learning what works and what does not; bringing about positive change and seeing the difference it is making; becoming more aligned internally and externally – all of these can lead to insights that can impact on a person's way of being. Those who adopt Effective Reflective Practice and use it consistently are likely to experience their lives in ways that are qualitatively different. Being more intentional in our professional roles will lead to being more thoughtful about many aspects of our lives. This, in turn, will support greater wellbeing. And once people are thriving or flourishing, they will have more to give to others, will be more open to engaging fully in reflective practice and will have the capacity to be kinder and more appreciative of others. These factors allow us to be fully present not only through the process of Effective Reflective Practice, but all the time. In many ways, it is not the learning, or the fact that we have changed, or that we are more aligned, it is this quality of presence that is experienced by our clients, making the biggest difference to those we serve.

## SUMMARY

In this chapter, we have surveyed the foundational principles of Effective Reflective Practice and explored four of its purposes. We asked you to start on your own reflective journey. Your reflective learning journal will be key to capturing and acknowledging what you are learning about reflective practice and yourself. If you have not already done so, we urge you to set aside some time now to get started. As we have argued, reflective practice is all about learning and change. There is no point learning *about* reflective practice solely as a theoretical subject.

### Find Out More

Boyatzis, R. (2006). An overview of intentional change from a complexity perspective. *Journal of Management Development* 25(7): 607-23.

Locke, E. A. & Latham, G. P. (2002). Building a practically useful theory of goal setting and task motivation. *American Psychologist* 57(9): 705-17.

# 3

# THE EFFECTIVE REFLECTIVE PRACTICE FRAMEWORK

This chapter will cover:

- The framework of Effective Reflective Practice
  - Intention
  - Outcome
  - Strategy
  - Experimentation
  - Evaluation
  - Insights
- An example of the framework in practice

Building on existing learning theories and reflective practice processes, we have set out a new framework for reflective practice. It responds to the increasing demand for effective strategies for supporting intentional change in professional contexts. We have integrated recent positive psychology theories and strategies to ensure an explicit focus on wellbeing. The Effective Reflective Practice framework comprises six stages. It aims to facilitate reflective practice that is impactful and effective. The framework is designed to make it easier to write about its application. It is our contention that reflective practice can only be considered *effective* if it leads to better outcomes for the professional, their clients and key stakeholders. In other words, it is more than a process of just *thinking* about professional practice. That is only part of it. The process of reflection should lead to improved professional practice, the improvements should be experienced by clients and stakeholders, and undertaking reflective practice must not be detrimental to the wellbeing of the professional.

## SETTING OUT THE FRAMEWORK

The Effective Reflective Practice framework (see Figure 3.1) encourages professionals to follow a cycle of Thinking, Planning, Acting and Reviewing. This cycle captures the purpose and intent of reflective practice. Within the cycle, there are six discrete stages that should be followed. When demonstrating Effective Reflective Practice in writing, professionals can describe their engagement with the cycle by providing a commentary about each of the stages described below.

**Figure 3.1** The Effective Reflective Practice framework

### Stage 1: Intention

The start of Effective Reflective Practice is a positive intention relating to one's professional practice. It is necessary to emphasise that the intention should be *positive* because the process of reflective practice is about making things better. When setting an intention, professionals are invited to think about a number of stakeholders. First, what is the positive intention towards clients or colleagues? It is important to resist the very normal inclination to focus solely on what the professional would like to change about themselves. The Effective Reflective Practice framework *starts* with others in mind: what would the professional like *others* to experience? Second, what does the professional hope will be better for their context or organisation? This is an invitation to think more broadly about the impact of any changes within the wider system. Third, what positive intention does the professional have for themselves? Once the intention has been clearly articulated, the last step before moving to the next stage is for the professional to reflect on their level of commitment to the intention. How committed are they? What is important to them about making this change?

## Stage 2: Outcome

The positive intention sets the scene and the basis for Effective Reflective Practice. As suggested above, it is important to ensure that there is likely to be sustained commitment to making things better. For Effective Reflective Practice, the desired outcome should be made as clear and explicit as possible. It is helpful to identify a situation, interaction or event that you would like to improve. The desired outcome should be set out positively. In other words, how would the professional like the situation, interaction or event to be in the future? This should be described in some detail, including how they will know the outcome has been achieved. What does success look like? Then it is helpful to consider how things are at present. Exploring how the professional would like things to be, and then taking some time to assess the current situation will raise awareness about what may need to happen to make progress. Once the gap between the current situation and desired future state has become clear, it is time to move to the next stage of the framework.

## Stage 3: Strategy

The strategy stage focuses on what the professional is going to *do* in order to move towards their desired outcome. The required actions should be specific and focused so that forward movement can happen and the results can be evaluated. The strategy should be aligned with the stakeholder and organisational interests identified in Stage 1, as well as with the professional's own values. The professional will benefit from considering the support needed from others in the system in order to implement the actions effectively. The following questions are important to consider:

- Who else needs to be consulted and involved?
- How will you go about engaging the interest and participation of others with diverse backgrounds, expertise and experience?
- What learning will you need to take the strategy forward, and how will this be acquired?

While the strategy should be aspirational, it should also comprise practical, implementable steps and include a contingency plan for any anticipated early setbacks based on reflection-in-advance.

## Stage 4: Experimentation

In implementing their strategy, the professional should be open to experimentation, trying out new ways of doing things. While the professional should be able to take calculated risks as part of experimenting, clients and other stakeholders must not be exposed to undue hazards or negative unintended consequences. Experimentation will help the professional be mindful of how well the implementation of their strategy is working, enabling them to make adjustments as they proceed. It will be essential to create space to stand back from the action and notice the thoughts and feelings that emerge as experiments progress. What is the professional learning about themselves in the process? Finding a way to record these reflections will enable the professional to recall these observations for use in later stages of this framework. Regular journaling to capture your current thinking, feelings and seemingly random impressions can prove very fruitful at this point in the process.

## Stage 5: Evaluation

This stage is about how the strategy has worked out in practice. Of crucial importance is the question of whether it has made a difference. At Stage 2, the professional will have established an idea of what a successful outcome would look like. This can be used as a starting point for evaluating how things have actually turned out. Some thought will be needed about what data will enable the professional to make a sound judgement. This is likely to include constructive feedback from others – clients, colleagues and other relevant stakeholders. These questions can be helpful for reflection:

- Does the review of progress suggest the need for further experimentation?
- What has been the impact for the client, the organisation and the professional themselves?
- Has the wellbeing of the people involved, including the professional, been maintained or improved?

## Stage 6: Insights

At this stage of the framework, the professional is able to capture the key learning points and insights from the process. This requires a review of the original intention, the identified outcome, the chosen strategy, the results of the experimentation and an evaluation of the whole process. In reviewing these stages, the learning that took place throughout the cycle should be captured and celebrated. This learning, along with any other insights, should be recorded, and will inform further improvements to professional practice. Throughout the cycle, and particularly at this final stage, it can be invaluable to have conversations with significant others who can act as a powerful sounding board to test out the professional's reflections and learning.

## Illustrative Case Study

Jasbir is a teacher of English in a school working with 15-year-old students. This is her first teaching post following graduation with a degree in English followed by a professional teaching certificate. Here are some extracts from her reflective diary.

### 1 October

Really struggling with one of the students in my class, B, who is not engaging with the content of the lesson – disrupting her own and others' learning. What to do?

### 3 October

(INTENTION – OWN & STAKEHOLDERS)

(THINK) I want to ensure B gets the most out of my classes and succeeds with her English exam. Talking with other teachers it's clear she is also disruptive in other lessons – though it seems not quite as much. If I can help her engage better, hopefully there will be a knock-on benefit for my colleagues too. Also need to crack this problem for myself – I need to be better at engaging with a wide range of students. No doubt I'll encounter similar problems with other groups – I need to be prepared. Really committed to making *something* work!

(PLAN) Talk to colleagues – what do they do? Read up about dealing with disruptive behaviour (google?).

(ACT) Raised the issue in a staff meeting. Colleagues helpful and supportive.

(REVIEW) Got some useful tips from colleagues and the internet – e.g. don't take it personally, tackle the behaviour not the personality. I'll bear these in mind.

### 4 October

Have B's class again today! Have to say I'm rather dreading it today. Not sure how much longer I can put up with B's bad behaviour ...

... Argh! – the lesson was awful. The lesson was focused on poetry and B was particularly disruptive. It's really getting to me. Affecting my motivation day-to-day.

*(Continued)*

## 5 October

(OUTCOME)

(THINK) Given a bit more thought to the issue - what would life be like if this issue were resolved? Would be great if B showed more interest in what I'm teaching, showed some progress with her learning - and just approached my lessons more calmly. Have to make sure she doesn't interfere with others' ability to engage. I need to feel I can handle this.

So what's causing the current issue?

- She's turned off by the lesson content (??)
- She's had enough of school and doesn't want to be here anymore (??)
- It's me! - my relationship with B is not right in some way (??). That would be very worrying.

(PLAN) Explore the situation with B.

(ACT) Have set up a conversation with B after next week's class.

(REVIEW) Feel good that I've taken a first step towards resolving things. Nothing's happened yet but it feels good to be at least trying to move forward.

## 7 October

(STRATEGY)

(THINK) ... so what are you going to do, J? Start with the 'lesson content' issue - that feels like something I can do something about more easily. It's important to me that all my students benefit from my teaching - down to me to be responsible for making that happen.

(PLAN) Key action points:

- Try to find out what's bugging her - really listen to what she has to say, and acknowledge her feelings
- Find out what interests her outside of school - make links to the lesson content?
- Spell out the impact of B's behaviour before reinforcing the expectations around appropriate behaviour (NB re-read school policy + google dealing with disruptive behaviour in class). Be firm about the expectations but help her to work out how *she* can meet those expectations.

What support do I need with this?

- Talk to my mentor
- Talk to my Head of Year
- Share my thinking with other affected colleagues.

Remember: this is not just *my* problem.

What's 'Plan B'? Say B doesn't engage in the conversation with me??:

- Get more senior colleagues involved (??) – want to try to avoid this – potentially weakens my position
- Involve her parents (??) – ditto, avoid this too ideally – might impact my relationship with B longer term.

## 10 October

(ACT) Took the plunge! Spoke to B after class today. She was a bit reluctant at first but when she realised I was listening and interested, she opened up a bit. Finds English lessons 'boring'. Not sure how 'stupid poems' are going to help her in her life. Told her I'd pretty much felt the same thing at one point at school. She mentioned in passing that she (and some of the other students in my class) are interested in rap music. They get together most days after school to make up lyrics. Was able to make the point that this is poetry – which rather surprised B and could see that made her think. Note to self: bring this into a lesson?? Then a useful conversation about behaviour. B could see the point I was making and agreed things needed to be different.

(REVIEW) Felt like a really useful conversation. B engaged (eventually) and made all the right noises about her behaviour – not convinced that will stick though, but let's see. Gained some valuable insight into B's interests.

## 17 October

(EXPERIMENTATION)

(THINK) It's time to take a few risks – give something new a go today.

(PLAN) Have planned a lesson on poetry. Main activity will be encouraging class to write their own poems in whatever style they fancy (including song/rap lyrics). Will use their creations as starting point for illustrating the emotional power of poetry – and its connection to real life.

(ACT) Was brave and stuck to the lesson plan. Got the class writing poetry and all the students seemed to enjoy it.

(REVIEW) B really got into it – got a bit wild when reading out loud to the class (!) but at least this disruption was out of exuberance not boredom. Could this be a break-through (??). Felt more confident and in control of things today. Still need to emphasise appropriate behaviours – so need to speak to B again about that (she was still a bit over the top at a couple of points!).

## 20 November

(EVALUATION)

(THINK) What did I set out to achieve? Here's my earlier diary note:

(*Continued*)

*'Would be great if B showed more interest in what I'm teaching, showed some progress with her learning - and just approached my lessons more calmly. Have to make sure she doesn't interfere with others' ability to engage. I need to feel I can handle this'.*

(PLAN) What info do I need to check my progress?

- My observations of B's behaviour - has it changed? Is she more engaged now?
- Colleagues' feedback about B in other classes
- Indications of a stronger relationship with B.

(ACT) Raised issue again in staff meeting and spoke to some colleagues individually. Re-read my notes about B's behaviour and engagement. Thought about the various conversations I've had with B over the last month.

(REVIEW) Colleagues have noticed an improvement. Plus B is definitely more engaged in my classes - contributing much more to discussions and her essays are generally more thought through indicating learning is taking place. Less disruptive, though she still has her moments! As for me - I'm feeling more connected with B, and also the whole class. Feel less anxious and more motivated.

### 27 November

(INSIGHTS)

So what have I learnt from all this? And how can I apply that in the future?

A conversation with my mentor helped me identify my learning points:

- My relationship with each student is the key - getting closer to B has been helpful. Going forwards need to make sure this isn't at the expense of relationships with other students, though.
- Having meaningful conversations with students strengthens relationships and gives insights into what makes them tick and how to enable them to access lesson content.
- Lesson planning is important - but so is thinking about how content *lands* with students. Have tended to focus on the planning, rather than the student experience.

I need to keep up the momentum that's been created. Under no illusions - B can still be a handful and will likely need continuing clear and consistent guidance about her behaviour.

## SUMMARY

In this chapter, we set out a new framework for reflective practice. It has been designed with two purposes in mind: undertaking reflective practice and demonstrating reflective practice through writing. In the following chapters, we will consider each of the six stages in more detail.

### Find Out More

For a sneak peek of a completed write-up of a piece of reflective writing, see Appendix 1 on p. 131.

# 4

# HOW TO IDENTIFY INTENTIONS AND OUTCOMES

This chapter will cover:

- Identifying the intention of Effective Reflective Practice
    - How to set a positive intention
- Being clear about the desired outcome of Effective Reflective Practice
    - How to determine a desired outcome
- Reviewing your values

**Figure 4.1** The Effective Reflective Practice framework (with Intentions and Outcomes highlighted)

## STARTING WITH THE END IN MIND: INTENTION

Effective Reflective Practice deliberately starts with intention. Positive intention is fundamental to Effective Reflective Practice because it provides the professional with a clear desired outcome whilst also connecting them to the purpose of their change process (making things better). Further, it is the positive intention that supplies much of the motivation for the change that is required. This stage of the framework has direct links to every part of the Effective Reflective Practice cycle. It will guide you as you identify and become more specific about the desired outcome. It can provide the energy to commit to changes in behaviour or thinking which are necessary for progress to be made. The experimentation stage is an opportunity for you to put your positive intention to the test. The evaluation stage assesses whether the experiment has led to the desired outcome. And as we shall explore in this chapter, the outcome is likely to be aligned to the positive intention which started it all. Finally, the insights phase is an opportunity to reflect on all the learning that has taken place as you manifest your positive intention. To put it another way, Effective Reflective Practice starts and ends with intention.

The intention and outcomes stages are closely interrelated. While the visual representation of the framework may create the impression that it is a clear, linear process, it is important to note that it can be used flexibly. At its best, the process is fluid and dynamic. This is why we will be considering both stages together in this chapter.

## BEING CLEAR ABOUT WHAT IS WANTED: OUTCOME

Let us start by being clear and explicit. The initial starting point is the intention, not the outcome. The intention is the reason that a process of change is considered. The outcome is the desired future state that occurs when your positive intention is realised. When we refer to intention, we like to specify that a *positive* intention is more likely to lead to sustained and sustainable change. In the same way, we propose that we should be considering *desired* outcomes. In other words, you should be clear about *what is wanted*. This is to ensure that you will be pursuing what are called *approach* goals. Approach goals are the opposite of *avoidance* goals. An approach goal is one that a person is moving towards. An avoidance goal focuses on what is *not* wanted (Elliot & Friedman, 2007). Avoidance goals can lead to changes in behaviour – but they are rarely motivational and can have a negative impact on your wellbeing. The obvious reason for this is that avoidance goals draw our attention to unpleasant situations, while approach goals require us to imagine desired future outcomes.

In Effective Reflective Practice, the first step is to identify a positive intention in relation to your professional practice. Once a broad, positive intention has been chosen, you are invited to imagine how this positive intention would be experienced by your clients and stakeholders. This is followed by reflecting on the impact it would have on you. This is what we refer to as the *desired outcome* – what will be positively different for your clients, your stakeholders and yourself?

## Questions for Consideration when Setting a Positive Intention

- What will be different in how others experience you?
- Who is likely to be most affected if you make this change?
- How will others know that you have made a change?
- What difference will this change make to you, personally?
- How will this positive intention support your professional growth?
- How might your intention improve the wider context in which you work?

Of course, the positive intention should inform the desired outcome. Defining the outcome is one way of operationalising the intention. To be sure, this is not a one-way interaction. Once you have identified the desired outcome, it is helpful to revisit the intention to ensure good alignment between the two. The process may lead you to refine or re-think your intention, which may then invite further reflection on the desired outcome. This is why we have presented these two stages together – they are interrelated. Positive intention comes from within: it is linked to your values, principles, strengths and aspirations. Outcomes are external representations of what is wanted. Defining these two elements at the start of the Effective Reflective Practice process will increase the chances of making improvements that will enhance the experience of your clients.

## Story from Practice: Setting and Re-setting Positive Intentions

One of the authors engaged in a process of reflective practice to improve their approach as an online course facilitator. When delivering in-person training, they had always allowed for informal chats and incidental conversations with delegates during coffee and lunch breaks. They would even take their time packing up so that delegates could interact with them after the course had ended. The author realised that those opportunities were absent during online training courses. This was a good topic for Effective Reflective Practice. The author started by defining their positive intention as 'to provide one-to-one time for delegates on online training programmes'. This seemed clear, and it was positive. They went on to

*(Continued)*

think about a specific desired outcome with the delegates in mind. They decided that the outcome would be 'that delegates would have access to 1-1 time at the end of online training programmes'. When the author revisited the intention, they realised that it did not fully capture what was motivating them to make the change. The author then revised the positive intention to 'That delegates of online training programmes are able to connect with me and feel valued'. This led to a slight revision of the desired outcome to: 'That delegates feel there is an opportunity for them to talk to me as the facilitator outside the formal part of the online training session'. This rewording was clearer and seemed achievable. More importantly, the positive intention was much more aligned to the author's values and was therefore more motivational.

Because these two stages set the direction and purpose of the reflective practice, it is important to invest time and energy exploring and refining your positive intention and desired outcome. The strategy and process of experimentation will only move you forward if they are based on a clear idea of what is wanted. Below, we will consider practical ways of identifying your intention and outcomes.

## GETTING PRACTICAL: WAYS OF IDENTIFYING YOUR INTENTIONS AND OUTCOMES

In this section, we present a few different ways to identify the intentions and outcomes you seek through Effective Reflective Practice. You may prefer to use or adapt frameworks and models you already know that achieve the same ends. The important thing is that you choose an approach that works well for you. It can be helpful to become comfortable with using your chosen method … *and* it can be useful to step outside this comfort zone to try something new to see if anything different emerges from working on things from another angle.

Underlying your intention are your core values, which have a powerful influence over how you think and behave. It is worth spending some time identifying your values as this will provide a foundation for establishing your intentions. You obviously will not need to do this every time you engage in Effective Reflective Practice. The more you become aware of your values, the less time you will need to spend on this activity. It is, however, worth revisiting your values periodically as they may shift over time.

## IDENTIFYING PERSONAL VALUES

Our values are defined as the principles that give our lives meaning. They influence how we live our lives, shaping how we respond to situations and how we set and prioritise outcomes. Our values are important to us and characterise who we are as individuals. They also underpin our interactions and relationships with others – and, indeed, our relationships with ourselves. For example, our values influence whether we believe life is going well because our values align with our experiences, or not so well because things are out of sync. While our core values tend to remain stable, they can change over time based on our life experiences, particularly in the aftermath of highly impactful events. There are tried and tested ways for identifying, or re-affirming, your values. We share six methods below.

## Method 1: Starting from a List of Values

You can start from a list of values such as the one we have provided here. Select the six values that resonate most with you. Make a note in your learning journal of these values. Can some of them be clustered together because they are similar or connected in some way? Is it possible to rank the values in order of their importance to you?

### Core Values

These values have been identified by a leading social psychologist (Schwartz, 2012). We have provided a brief explanation of each in Table 4.1.

**Table 4.1** Schwartz's core values

| Value | People who have this value |
|---|---|
| Self-direction | Exhibit freedom of thought and action; are self-motivated |
| Stimulation | Enjoy life; seek out challenges; like to engage in new activities |
| Hedonism | Enjoy experiences; focus on achieving personal pleasure |
| Achievement | Get recognition through externally-validated success |
| Power | Enjoy being in control and having authority |
| Security | Seek safety and harmony; appreciate stability |
| Conformity | Meet social expectations and norms; avoid causing upset |
| Tradition | Appreciate maintaining customs and following cultural norms |
| Benevolence | Are kind to people and concerned about the welfare of others |
| Universalism | Concerned with the fairness of society and the human impact on nature |

## Method 2: Using a Personal Inventory

The Values-in-Action (VIA) Strengths Inventory (Peterson & Seligman, 2004) generates a ranked list of values-based personal strengths. As with all such inventories, the profile produced is intended to provide you with some information about yourself which can stimulate your thinking.

## Method 3: Identifying the Values of the People you Respect and Admire

Select four people from your work or private life, who have, or have had, a significant impact on you. What are the values that you admire in the ways they think, feel and behave? An alternative approach is to consider the values exhibited by the actions of your role models. What are the values that have drawn you to these people?

## Method 4: Revisiting Significant Moments in your Work and Life

Major events in our lives, both painful and joyous, can be occasions when we reveal what we value most.

- When were you most successful?
- When were you most proud?
- When were you most fulfilled and satisfied?
- When did things go badly wrong?
- When were you most dissatisfied with things at work or in life?

Thinking back to these significant moments, what do they tell you about the values you hold dear?

## Method 5: Reflect on Your Deeply-held Beliefs

Determine key values based on your philosophy of life, taking into account your faith, religion, spiritual beliefs or worldview. What does this tell you about living according to your values? How can you incorporate these insights into your reflective practice?

## Method 6: Notice Your Choices

Over the course of a week notice how you make decisions and keep a note in your journal to record the values you are using to inform them.

- How do the values you have identified play out in your life?
- What other values might be influencing how you go about your work and life?
- Which values are you happy for the world to know you by?
- Looking back over your week, to what extent do you feel you are living up to your values?

- Do you need to re-evaluate your list of core values – or find different ways to make sure others experience your chosen values more strongly?

## IDENTIFYING INTENTION AND OUTCOME

Take a large piece of paper and a selection of coloured pens or markers.

Start by marking out the paper as shown in Figure 4.2 – creating four large rectangles representing stakeholders, organisational context, yourself and your commitment.

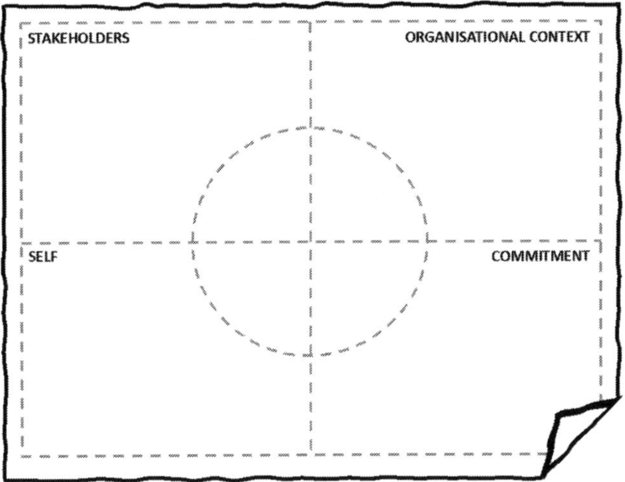


**Figure 4.2** Identifying intention and outcome: Overview

The circle at the centre of the diagram represents your intentions in each of the four areas. The four rectangles are for recording the outcomes you seek in each area. As discussed earlier in this chapter, your intentions and outcomes are interconnected.

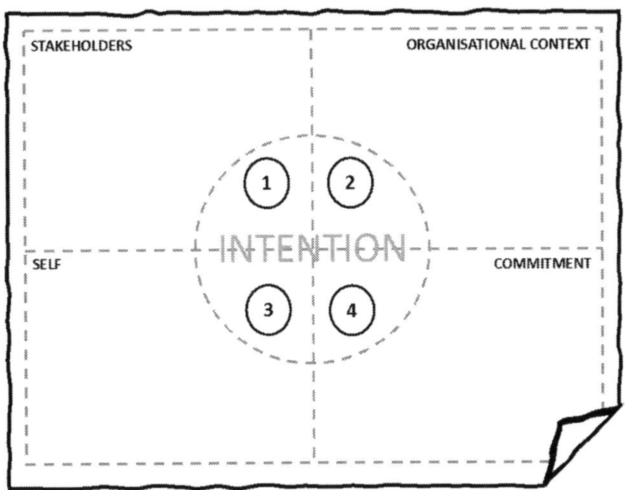


**Figure 4.3** Identifying intention and outcome: Inner circle

Focusing in on the topic you have identified for reflection, and starting with 'Intention' and 'Stakeholders' populate part 1 of the circle (see Figure 4.3) with answers to the following questions:

- Who are the stakeholders in this situation? There may, of course, only be one but test your assumptions about the people who are really impacted. Are some stakeholders more important than others? Why?
- What is your positive intention towards each of the stakeholders you have identified? Have you paid sufficient attention to their unique characteristics based on, for example, their race, gender or neurotype? Note that it is vital not to make assumptions about any of these characteristics and that no-one can be an 'expert' on every facet of human existence. Are some of your stakeholders from under-represented or minoritised groups? Where appropriate, it will be preferable to enable stakeholders to speak for themselves. Finally, make sure you take into account any ethical questions you might face and, in particular the ethical standards your profession expects you to maintain.

Now move to the part 2 of the circle (see Figure 4.3) and plot:

- What organisations and organisational contexts are you and your stakeholders operating within?
- What is your positive intention regarding the impact you seek in these organisational settings?

Focusing on yourself in part 3 of the circle:

- What aspects of your professional practice are relevant to the intentions you have already identified?
- What is your positive intention about the benefits of change for yourself and your practice? For example, what are your hopes for your learning and growth?

Part 4 of the circle focuses on your level of commitment:

- What is your level of commitment to following through on your intentions?

Having clarified your positive intention, it is time to move on to exploring and deciding the outcomes you aim to achieve as a result. In each case you are encouraged to think about what success would look like.

Focus on the top-left rectangle (5) and outcomes for stakeholders (Figure 4.4):

- What positive change or improvement are you seeking that will fulfil your intention towards your stakeholders?

Turning to the organisational context rectangle (6):

- What outcome are you aiming for that will result in a positive difference being achieved in the organisational context in which you are working?

Rectangle 7 is where you need to explore and record the outcomes for your practice and continuing professional development:

- What outcome will you put in place for your own professional learning and development?

Finally, turn to rectangle 8, which focuses on your commitment to achieve the outcomes you have established.

- What is your motivation for achieving these outcomes?
- On a scale of 1 to 10, where 10 is high, where do you place your level of commitment to making the outcomes a reality? If this is less than 10, what factors – in your stakeholders, organisational contexts or yourself – are affecting your level of commitment? What would it take to move your commitment one point up the scale?

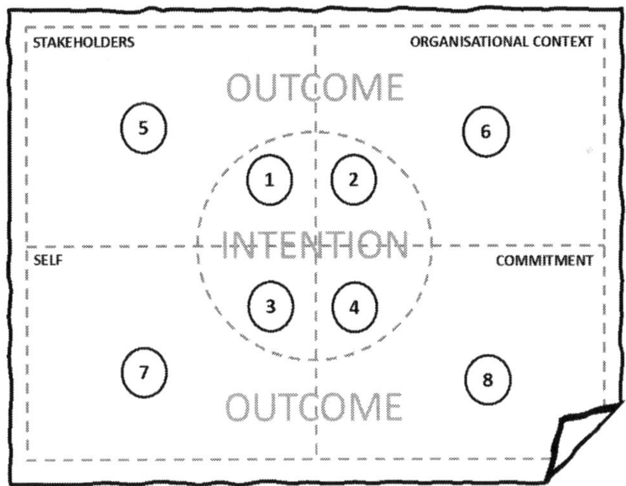


**Figure 4.4** Identifying intention and outcome: Outer rectangles

## SUMMARY

In this chapter, we have argued that the starting point for Effective Reflective Practice is a positive intention. To determine this, we have suggested that it is helpful to gain clarity about your values. The chapter explains how outcome and intention are inextricably connected and we have presented a framework for gaining clarity about your intention and outcomes and the relationship between them. We should note that the establishment of outcomes should not become too burdensome a process. You need to take account of the significance of the topic you are reflecting upon.

## Find Out More

Elliot, A. J. & Friedman, R. (2007). Approach-avoidance: A central characteristic of personal goals. In B. R. Little, K. Salmela-Aro & S. D. Phillips (Eds.), *Personal Project Pursuit: Goals, Actions, and Human Flourishing* (pp. 97–118). Mahwah, NJ: Lawrence Erlbaum.

Peterson, C. & Seligman, M. (2004). *Character Strengths and Virtues: A Handbook and Classification.* Oxford: Oxford University Press.

Schwartz, S. H. (2012). An overview of the Schwartz theory of basic values. *Online Readings in Psychology and Culture 2*(1).

# 5

# HOW TO PLAN AND EXPERIMENT

This chapter will cover:

- Developing a plan
  - Using a creative approach
  - Including your strengths
  - Identifying hypotheses
  - Clarifying outcomes
  - Considering the wider system
  - Code of Ethics
  - Equality Impact Assessment
- Experimenting
  - Practical guidance
  - Example of an experiment

**Figure 5.1** The Effective Reflective Practice framework (with Planning and Experimenting highlighted)

## PLANNING

Having identified your intention and decided on the outcome you are seeking, it is time to move on to planning how you propose to go about achieving the desired result. You have established the rationale for your reflective practice (i.e. the 'why' of your deliberations) which will give you a clear sense of purpose and the motivation to stay committed. The plan you create at this stage will form the basis of the experimentation that you will undertake to test out your ideas.

There will be varying degrees of complexity involved in creating your plan. Some outcomes will require detail and significant levels of thought, while others will offer a simple and obvious route through to fruition. While the latter may seem straightforward in terms of the thinking required, even they should be given careful consideration because there may be more involved than at first meets the eye. A clear plan will minimise the likelihood that your endeavours will be derailed at a later point in the reflective process.

If your reflective practice is connected to gaining a qualification or further professional credentialing, it would be a good idea to include a look at Chapter 7 where we discuss writing up your reflections for this purpose. This will help to ensure your plan includes the crucial elements required of you for certification.

Action plans are outlines of all the things you can think of that need to be in place for your outcome to be achieved. They are different from a 'to do' list which simply captures a list of random tasks that need to be accomplished within a specific timeframe. A plan will give you a clear framework outlining your initial 'best guess' for how to achieve your outcome successfully. As you implement your plan, perhaps through experimenting with different approaches, you can reflect on the effectiveness of your original thinking and adjust your plan to accommodate any emerging developments. As we have already discussed, the learning and insights you gain as you do this are an important part of Effective Reflective Practice.

Start your planning by thinking creatively about all the things that need to happen for your outcome to be achieved. The next step involves placing them in the sequence required for your actions to work effectively. Using sticky notes or online creativity tools can be a helpful, and freeing, way of capturing and sequencing your plan.

### A Creative Approach Using Sticky Notes

1 Generate as many thoughts as possible about the key points your plan needs to include without being concerned with the order in which they need to be undertaken or the priority that might be placed on them.
2 Capture these points on sticky notes using a different note for each one. It can be useful to use flipchart markers or felt-tipped pens; larger

writing makes it easier to read the sticky notes as they are generated and displayed. In addition, the sizes of the sticky notes and pen tips help to constrain the number of words that can be written, meaning each action point will be captured succinctly.

3 It can be helpful to record the emotional elements that arise as these may have an impact on your levels of motivation and commitment and may therefore need your consideration.
4 Think as broadly and deeply as you can about the outcome you are wanting to achieve so that you are creating a rich picture of all the elements involved. When you think you have finished, engage in at least one more round of thinking.
5 A number of themes or sub-themes may begin to emerge during the previous step and different coloured sticky notes or pens can be used to differentiate them. For example, you may discover you can cluster systemic factors that start to suggest connections. However, the points may emerge in a random fashion and patterns may not become clear until you have finished unpacking all the action points.
6 Display your sticky notes and cluster them according to relevant themes. What do you see emerging about the actions needed to achieve your outcome? Be careful not to accept the first thing you think of - put more thought into each of the clustered themes and their contents. Question your perceptions and assumptions. What is emerging that will further improve your plan?
7 Depending on the complexity of your outcome, you may need to undertake a number of clusterings before you gain a deeper understanding and are then able to identify ways forward.
8 You might wish to photograph your clusters of sticky notes to keep a record of your thinking and decision-making.

This activity can work well as an individual exercise and could also be undertaken with a colleague or a small group of people. There are sometimes benefits to thinking aloud with others about your choices.

## USING YOUR STRENGTHS

Effective Reflective Practice is a way of enhancing professional practice by focusing on the good: imagining what's wanted; identifying a positive outcome; and ultimately making this better. When developing your plans, it makes sense to harness the skills, resources and strengths you already have. The academic field of positive psychology has been researching human strengths for over two decades. Two leading positive psychologists (Peterson & Seligman, 2004) identified 24 universal character strengths. Each one of us has these strengths in different degrees. Knowing your strengths and using them regularly has been shown to boost your confidence, enhance your wellbeing and strengthen your relationships (VIA Institute on Character).

### 24 Universal Character Strengths

- Creativity (adaptive)
- Curiosity (seeking novelty)
- Judgement (open-mindedness)
- Love of learning (mastering new skills)
- Perspective (wisdom)
- Honesty (authenticity)
- Bravery (courage)
- Perseverance (persistence)
- Zest (enthusiasm)
- Kindness (generosity)
- Love (loving and being loved)
- Social intelligence (emotional intelligence)
- Fairness (unbiased)
- Leadership (influential)
- Teamwork (citizenship)
- Forgiveness (merciful)
- Humility (modest)
- Prudence (cautious)
- Self-regulation (self-control)
- Appreciation of beauty (admiration)
- Gratitude (thankful)
- Hope (optimistic)
- Humour (playful)
- Spirituality (religiousness)

The first step is to know and acknowledge your own strengths. You can get a good idea of your strengths by considering the strengths listed above. You can also complete a free survey of your strengths by visiting www.viacharacter.org. Once you are aware of your strengths, make sure to deploy them in your plan. As they are your strengths, you are naturally good at them. Using your strengths will be good for your levels of energy, motivation and wellbeing too.

## DEVELOPING A ROBUST ACTION PLAN

The plan will be your guide as you put your ideas into practice. It is therefore important to invest time in this part of the process. When developing your plan, keep in mind these tips and strategies:

- Include a clear representation of your desired outcome
- Specify the actions needed for your outcome to be achieved (it can be helpful to begin each activity with a verb to emphasise the need to take action)
- Identify who else will need to be considered (e.g. a client, other people with a stake in the outcome and/or colleagues who can provide you with specified areas of support)
- Set out a timescale outlining the sequence of activities and their prioritisation
- Determine an end date for the achievement of your desired outcome
- Highlight critical milestones along the way that will help to check you are on track
- List the resources you will need in order to implement your plan.

You will need to scale the extent of your planning to fit with the complexity of the outcome you are seeking. This is to avoid the risk of 'paralysis by analysis' – getting so caught up in analysis and planning that you never get around to putting your ideas into action! Some level of 'not knowing' or vagueness at the start is acceptable. Your plan should be a live, flexible document which provides a sense of direction, becomes an evolving guide to progress and a motivational aid to keep you committed to a successful outcome. Adopting a Plan–Do–Review mindset ensures that your plan remains relevant, allowing you to acknowledge and celebrate successes as they occur. As soon as you start implementing your plan you will be having an impact on the context you are working in, which may require adjustments to your thinking and approach. Even the most well-designed plans need to be adapted as the context changes.

### A Word of Caution

If you are 100% sure of your plan, it is worth taking a step back for a moment. Being that sure may mean your plan is too rigid and not sufficiently flexible to adapt to changing circumstances. The plan does not need to be perfect. In fact, it is highly likely to require adaptation and change as you learn more about what is needed. More important than 'getting the plan exactly right' is to invest time in thinking things through. Events will not go exactly as planned but the more you prepare the better able you are to think on your feet and make the necessary adjustments.

You can capture your plan using different formats – choose the method with which you feel most comfortable and supports you in your reflective endeavours. For example, you might decide to present your plan as a flowchart, a Gantt chart, a table or a spreadsheet.

## CLARIFYING OUTCOMES: THE SMARTER WAY

A tried and trusted way of crystallising outcomes is the SMARTER approach, an extension of the classic SMART method, which encourages thinking about the detail of an outcome or goal. SMART outcomes are specific with sufficient granularity to narrow the focus and guide your actions, clarifying the end result. They are measurable in ways that will enable you to know the outcome has been achieved and also help you to know that you are headed in the right direction as you progress. It is important that outcomes are achievable – it is not helpful to be setting outcomes that are not feasible in the circumstances. However, the outcome should have a 'stretch' element, rather than simply accepting the status quo, and might be designed to challenge the current reality. SMART outcomes need to be relevant. This can involve relevance to various factors – for example, benefits for stakeholders, building your own capability and/or impacts on the organisational context. The 'T' in SMART refers to time and enables you to establish an appropriate timescale in which the outcome is to be achieved. This timescale should be reasonable in the context, meaning it needs to allow sufficient space for the outcome to be achieved without being so far into the future that the activity loses relevance.

Later versions of the SMART model include two additional factors which are helpful to consider. The 'E' in the SMARTER framework refers to evaluation. It encourages thinking about how progress will be reviewed along the way so you have a means of checking that the outcome remains on track. The final 'R' in the SMARTER approach focuses on reviewing progress and points to the possibility that it may need to be amended in the light of emerging circumstances.

It is worth considering the level of detail required for your plan. Bear in mind that while all goals are outcomes, not all outcomes are goals. So, if you have a specific outcome with a clear solution that you want to focus on in your reflections establishing a SMARTER goal will be beneficial and will help you to maintain your focus and energy, turning new behaviours into habitual routines.

If, however, you don't know what a solution would look like, or simply want to explore to see what emerges, tying things down too tightly is likely to be a distraction. Instead, being more open to not knowing, and the exploration and emergence that accompanies your 'unknowing' will enable ideas to bubble up. This is how things can work for some people. In fact, tapping into your own creativity or using creative techniques can be very helpful ways to build motivation and generate insights (see Chapter 9).

## THINKING ABOUT THE WIDER SYSTEM

Throughout this book we are encouraging you to always keep in mind the wider context in which you are working. An obvious person to keep at the forefront of your Effective Reflective Practice is your client. There may also be other stakeholders who stand to gain (or not) by your actions. In any case, the wider system in which you and your stakeholders are operating will have helping and hindering impacts on the achievement of your outcome. The factors driving those impacts need to be considered for a successful outcome to be achieved.

A STEEPLEE analysis can help you to think about specific features of the wider system that are in play. Which of the factors listed in Table 5.1 might be prevalent in the situation you are exploring?

**Table 5.1** STEEPLEE analysis

| |
|---|
| **Social:** Who is involved and what are their connections? What aspects of the organisational culture and the context you are working in impact the topic you are focusing on? |
| **Technological:** What technological factors affect the situation? |
| **Economic:** What financial, and other resources, are available to support the activity? |
| What monetary constraints might be problematic? |
| **Environmental:** What factors related to the climate emergency are involved? How might your outcome strengthen sustainability? |
| **Political:** What macro and micro driving forces are impacting the situation? |
| **Legal:** What legal obligations need to be taken account of (including organisational policy implications and accepted professional standards and expectations)? |
| **Equity:** What are the relative position and power of the people involved? How might your outcome enhance inclusion and diversity in your work? How will you avoid making assumptions based on stereotypes related to race, gender and gender identification, disability, neurotype, expertise, experience or any other factor that might lead you to draw inappropriate and inaccurate conclusions about people? (See box below) |
| **Ethical:** What are the (actual and potential) ethical dimensions and their implications? Ethical behaviour is the manifestation of your values, and those of any organisation with which you are involved. Clients and stakeholders will draw conclusions about your values based on the ethics of your behaviour, rather than, say, those espoused in any formal Values Statements. Ethical issues are always complex, requiring management, rather than problems with a simple, once-and-for-all solution. |

## CODE OF ETHICS AND EQUALITY IMPACT ASSESSMENT

Effective Reflective Practice is a process of bringing about positive changes to your professional practice and being more aware of its impact on others and the wider environment.

Once you have identified key elements of your plan, and before you move to the experimentation stage, you should check that your proposed actions are ethical. Even with the best intentions, there is a risk that something that you are planning to do may inadvertently cause harm to people or be discriminatory.

### Code of Ethics

When ensuring that your plan is ethical, you should refer to a Code of Ethics that is appropriate to your professional role. There may be variations between codes of ethics or expected requirements of professional practice, but broadly speaking they will include:

- not seeking to harm others
- trying to do the 'right' thing
- adhering to the laws that apply in your location
- having the best interest of clients in mind
- working within your area of professional competence.

### Equality Impact Assessment

This assessment is undertaken to ensure that the actions proposed in your plan do not inadvertently discriminate against certain individuals or groups of people. Could your experiment negatively impact your clients or anyone else involved? Take special care to consider the impact of your proposed actions on people from marginalised communities, neurodivergent people, minority ethnic groups and diverse populations. Look through your plans for any negative assumptions you are making about your client(s) due to their background or identity. For example, what assumptions might you be making that are based on your limited knowledge of a client's background? It is worth remembering that ultimately your client is the 'expert' on how factors in their background shape the intricacies of how they experience the world. It is also important to be aware of how your proposed changes may adversely affect certain groups of people. (Appendix 4 provides more details about how to carry out an EIA on your plan.)

Once you have tested your plan against the Code of Ethics and undertaken an EIA, you should make any necessary amendments. You should not proceed to the experimentation stage until you are confident that the actions in your plan are both ethical and fair.

## EXPERIMENTING

Once your plans are in place, it is time to move to the exciting stage of putting them into practice. Acknowledging everything that we have discussed about the importance of taking context into account, it is helpful to think of this stage as one of 'experimentation'. In Effective Reflective Practice, this is the point at which you adopt the stance of a 'scientist practitioner' (Peterson & Park, 2006) who researches their development and then uses the findings from their research to inform future growth. In the experimentation stage, you undertake experiments, collect data and observe what happens when you try different things.

The notion of experimentation allows us to celebrate the process of learning through trial and error. In this case, the trials have been created in the earlier 'planning' stage. The experimentation stage involves putting these trials into practice.

When these trials do not lead to the outcomes we want, this can be understood as 'positive failure'. Positive failure is defined as 'a failure after appropriate investment that leads to further learning or development' (Arnott, 2013, p. 4). According to positive psychologists, 'a dose of failure is like being vaccinated – while not initially pleasant, it can be good over the long term because trying and failing can lead to development and growth. And it is in this sense that a dose of failure can be embraced – through a focus on the learning that comes from the experience and doing things differently next time' (Jarden & Jarden, 2022, pp. 128–9). In other words, while there is always learning taking place during experiments, you are likely to learn more through positive failure than if everything goes according to plan.

During the experimentation stage, you are simultaneously putting your plan into practice and being curious about the extent to which your plan is working. Rather than simply implementing the plan regardless of what happens, the experimentation stage ensures that you are learning at the same time. This new learning is an important part of Effective Reflective Practice.

## Getting Practical

The first step of this stage is to formulate no more than three hypotheses based on your action plan. A hypothesis is used as a starting point for research based on prior knowledge, experience or observations. It is an educated guess or a prediction about the relationship between two or more variables. Hypotheses are therefore often presented as 'if/then' statements. The purpose of experiments is to test the hypothesis to determine whether it is valid or not.

### How Hypotheses are used in Scientific Experiments

1. Researchers start by identifying the problem or question that they would like to investigate.
2. Researchers formulate a hypothesis that tentatively explains the relationship between the variables in question.
3. Researchers develop an experimental design that allows them to test the hypothesis.
4. Researchers collect and analyse data to determine whether the hypothesis is supported or not.
5. Researchers draw conclusions based on the data collected and revise the hypothesis if necessary.
6. Researchers write up the findings of their research so that the findings can be of use to themselves and others.

It is important to note that a hypothesis is, by definition, a tentative explanation for a phenomenon – the opposite of a 'fact'. To get the most out of hypotheses, it is necessary to remain very open-minded and willing to revise your hypothesis based on what you learn through experimentation. Being prepared to challenge your assumptions, about the people involved, the situation you are exploring and the context in which it takes place, is an essential part of being open-minded. If your hypothesis turns out to be valid, then you have learnt that you are headed in the right direction, and you should proceed with your plans. If the hypothesis is not supported through your experiment, then you should reflect on what you have learnt. There will be valuable learning and insights from every experiment. Following a period of reflection, you will need to develop a new hypothesis and go through the process again.

## Example of Hypothesis

- Initial hypothesis: 'If I were to offer 30 minutes of "informal time" at the end of coach training workshops delivered through Zoom, it would lead to attendees feeling safer and more valued.'

However, hypotheses need to be testable and falsifiable. In the above hypothesis, it would be difficult to determine whether attendees felt safe and more valued without follow-up surveys. So it was broken down into two hypotheses:

- Hypothesis 1: 'If I were to offer 30 minutes of "informal time" at the end of coach training workshops, at least 10% of the participants would stay on to take advantage of the opportunity.'
- Hypothesis 2: 'Those who stay on for the additional time would give positive feedback about the opportunity when asked.'

It was decided to start with these two hypotheses before addressing the question of whether the intervention would lead to participants feeling more valued, which was the original intention.

As part of the experimentation, the facilitator selected three upcoming workshops and emailed participants to explain that the sessions would start at 9:00am and conclude formally at 1:00pm as originally advertised. The facilitator noted that they would make themselves available for a further 30 minutes from 1:00pm till 1:30pm. There were no responses from any of the participants. At the start of the workshop, the facilitator went through the schedule, highlighting the availability of an extra 30 minutes of informal time at the end. The facilitator explicitly said that it could be used to ask any questions that participants might be uncomfortable to share in front of the whole group or to discuss anything that was particular to individual participants. The facilitator reminded participants of that opportunity just before the lunch break. Finally, the facilitator ended the formal workshop at 1:00pm, inviting anyone who wanted to ask any further questions to stay on the Zoom meeting.

These were the results of the experiment:

## Workshop 1

Out of 18 participants, no participants stayed on after 1:00pm. (Hypothesis 1 is not supported)

There was no-one to ask for feedback. (Not enough information for Hypothesis 2)

## Workshop 2

Out of eight participants, no participants stayed on after 1:00pm. (Hypothesis 1 is not supported)

There was no-one to ask for feedback. (Not enough information for Hypothesis 2)

## Workshop 3

Out of the 15 participants, three participants stayed on after 1:00pm. (Hypothesis 1 is supported)

Out of the three participants who stayed on after 1:00pm, all three noted their appreciation of the availability of extra time. (Hypothesis 2 is supported)

When the facilitator considered the results, they realised that the assumption that the opportunity would be consistently taken up was inaccurate. However, when people did stay on, they reported that they appreciated the time. These results were helpful for the facilitator, who concluded that making such time available was perceived to be useful by those who were likely to take it up – but not all. The experience also made it evident to the facilitator that the invitation to stay on at the end of the formal time meant that the ending of the session was less clear cut – leading to some awkwardness at the end. Based on the mixed results, the facilitator decided to adapt the intervention. In future, the facilitator would offer the opportunity to request additional time during the lunch break. Anyone who wanted to stay on would need to send a direct message to the facilitator who would invite them to join the 1:00pm–1:30pm additional time.

The new hypotheses were:

- Hypothesis 1: 'Anyone who requests additional time will give positive feedback about the opportunity when asked.'
- Hypothesis 2: 'The majority of people who attend the workshop and respond to a post-workshop survey will answer positively to the question "I felt that I was valued as a participant and had opportunity to ask as many questions as I wanted".'

Both of these were supported in the next three workshops, leading the facilitator to adopt this approach thereafter.

Experimentation is as much a mindset as it is a stage in the process for Effective Reflective Practice. This chapter has set out how to develop hypotheses and test them in your professional contexts. However, the essence of the 'experimental mindset' simply calls for openness to experience, curiosity and flexibility in the face of possible setbacks and frustrations. So, for those of you who prefer to keep things simple, you do not need to develop and test hypotheses. Instead, you could just come up with a question about your practice and then look for answers by trying out different things. For example, 'I wonder whether offering extra time at the end of workshops might make participants feel more valued?' Adopting the experimental mindset whilst trying to answer your question would mean that you would accept challenges and difficult experiences you encounter as part of the process of discovery. In other words, you would appreciate the learning and insights that emerge as you look for answers to your question. Whichever route you select for your experimentation, you are choosing to put into practice carefully designed plans to move towards your intention and desired outcome with the understanding that there will be rich and useful learning along the way.

## SUMMARY

In this chapter we have covered two of the key components of Effective Reflective Practice – planning and experimentation. As you will have noticed, the two are closely connected. Experimentation without careful planning would be wasted effort. On the other hand, excellent plans that are not put into practice have no effect. Starting with a meaningful understanding of your intention and a clear sense of your desired outcome, you are then able to develop a plan that is appropriate for you and the context you are in. Once that plan is in place, you can start to try things out. Through an iterative process of hypothesising and testing your assumptions, you will learn more about what will work best for you and your clients in your particular situation. The next chapter will explore the review phase, where you will be invited to look back over the entire reflective practice process to determine how successful you have been in bringing your intention to life and to reflect on what has been learnt along the way.

### Find Out More

Arnott, A. (2013). *Positive Failure: Understand How Embracing Failure is a Tool for Development*. Liverpool: Liverpool Academic Press.

Jarden, A. & Jarden, R. (2022). Learn about yourself. In C. van Nieuwerburgh & P. Williams (Eds.), *From Surviving to Thriving: A Student's Guide to Feeling and Doing Well at University* (pp. 127–38). London: Sage.

Niemec, R. M. & McGrath, R. E. (2019). *The Power of Character Strengths*. Cincinnati, OH: VIA Institute on Character.

Peterson, C. & Park, N. (2006). Character strengths in organizations. *Journal of Organizational Behavior, 27*: 1149-54.

Peterson, C. & Seligman, M. (2004). *Character Strengths and Virtues: A Handbook and Classification*. Oxford: Oxford University Press.

# 6

# HOW TO REVIEW THE PROCESS AND THE LEARNING

This chapter will cover:

- An explanation of the review phase
- What to think about during this phase
- Learning theories that will support this phase
    - Kolb's learning cycle
    - Argyris's double loop learning
    - Bruner's constructivist theory
    - Myers-Briggs Type Indicator
    - VARK learning styles
- How to capture your thoughts and insights

**Figure 6.1** The Effective Reflective Practice framework (with Review and Learning highlighted)

The review and learning phases evaluate the effectiveness of the process and bring together all the learning that has been gained to this point. To get the most value from the process, the review component should be clear and concise. The review and learning phases are the most structured of the Effective Reflective Practice cycle. This is to ensure that the process is as valuable as possible to the reflective practitioner. The review phase should be initiated on the date identified in your plan or when you believe that you have achieved a result that is close to your desired outcome. In some cases, it may be necessary to start the review process when it becomes clear that the desired outcome may not be possible within particular contexts, circumstances or timescales.

## THE REVIEW PHASE

The review phase is best undertaken individually or with one other person. The first two questions to consider are:

1 Has the outcome been achieved for the client?
2 Have you achieved your desired outcome?

In answering these questions, it is helpful to provide 'yes' or 'no' answers. When the answer is 'yes', write down the evidence to support your judgement in your learning journal. When the answer is 'no', jot down some notes about the barriers to achieving the outcomes.

The third question to ask may initially seem counterintuitive:

3 If you did achieve the outcomes, to what extent do they align with your original intention?

In the course of pursuing outcomes, it is possible that we lose sight of our intentions. In some cases, we may find that we have met the outcomes but we are no closer to our original intention. For example, let us imagine that a leader's intention was to encourage more risk-taking in their organisation by co-designing safe spaces for their team to meet and discuss ideas. Even if a meeting room were earmarked as a space for creative discussions and it was used regularly by the members of the team as a safe space to chat and throw ideas around, it may not have led to more risk-taking. One could even imagine scenarios in which the opportunity to talk more regularly with colleagues might even lead to team members 'playing it safe' more often. This is why it is necessary to check whether the positive outcomes continue to be aligned with your original intention.

In ideal scenarios, you may be able to answer 'yes' to all three questions. This means that the process of Effective Reflective Practice has been successful in bringing about desired change. However, we should note that this is only one part of the purpose of reflective practice. The other part is to learn through practice and use the new knowledge to further enhance the positive impact that you are having on others. In fact, even if you answer 'no' to the first two questions, Effective Reflective Practice means that there will be rich learning to take away and build into your future learning and development.

## Learning and Insights

If your outcomes have been achieved and your intention met, it is time to move on to capturing the learning that has taken place. What worked particularly well for you? What led to your success? This learning should be captured and can be used in future to further your personal and professional practice. On the other hand, if outcomes were not achieved or your intention was not met, there will still be rich learning that is worth reflecting upon. What assumptions about the people involved, the situation and the context did you make or were implicit? What challenges will need to be overcome? How can you design future cycles of Effective Reflective Practice to increase the chances of positive outcomes? In either case, after reviewing the success of the reflective practice, you should methodically capture the learning that has taken place since the start of the cycle. Addressing the questions below is a good way of doing this.

- How motivational was the positive intention? What did you learn about yourself in setting the intention? How closely aligned was your positive intention with your own purpose and values?
- How achievable were the outcomes? Were they the right outcomes to deliver on your intention? Now that you are coming to the end of the Effective Reflective Practice cycle, what are your reflections on the outcomes that you chose?
- Looking back at the plan, what worked well? What have you learnt about using your strengths? Were there any parts of the plan that were less useful?
- How good were you at sticking to the plan? Did you need to make any adaptations along the way? What ethical issues emerged – and how did you deal with them? What implications arose that impacted equality and inclusion outcomes? Knowing what you know now, would you change anything about the plan if you were to do it again?
- What was the most important learning you took away from the experimentation phase? What did you learn about yourself or your clients as you experimented? What worked particularly well? What elements may need further revision?

## What Next?

As we have said from the outset, reflective practice is only effective when it leads to desired change. Whatever the outcomes, it is imperative that you capture your learning in some way – audio recordings, vlogs, journal entries, free writing, etc. If you need to formally submit your reflective practice cycle, the next chapter will set out how to write this up for the purposes of assessment or evaluation. Then comes an even more important part: how will you use this learning? Will you start another cycle of Effective Reflective Practice in order to move closer to your original intention? Will you focus on turning the new behaviours into habits? Will you set new objectives and start a fresh cycle of Effective Reflective Practice to build on your successes? The more we learn about ourselves, our clients and our craft, the more questions will arise. Each cycle of Effective Reflective Practice is part of a greater, continuous process of learning, growth, appreciation and development.

## WHAT TO THINK ABOUT DURING YOUR REVIEW AND LEARNING PROCESS

### Yourself – Motivation

Considering your levels of motivation as you implemented your reflective practice plan can be a very important source of learning. At what points in the process did your motivation peak, or wane? What were the specific factors that energised you or caused you to lose interest or heart? In addition to the impact these fluctuations in motivation may have for your intended outcome, more generally, there may be valuable reflections here that offer insights about you as a human being and how you show up in your professional role. It can be helpful to think about what you found easy or difficult and reflect on how this made you feel.

### The Client

Throughout this book we are emphasising that central to Effective Reflective Practice is the achievement of improved outcomes for clients. While you will gain a great deal personally from the process, this needs to translate into changes that benefit clients. So your review and learning activity should focus on the impact on your client. Your original intention might have centred on a particular client around a specific issue, or it may have had a broader focus on something that would benefit a set of clients or contexts and circumstances in which clients find themselves. In any case, there will be beneficial insights that you can use to inform your practice with all your clients.

So it will be important to review how your client responded to your intended outcome and plan. Did they respond well or not so well? What caused that response? What feedback did you seek from the client about their response, how they felt and the impact your actions had on them? Clearly, gaining client feedback is invaluable. However, there is a risk of overwhelming the client. Requesting too much feedback about multiple aspects of your professional approach risks interfering with the very reason you are working together. It can be received as prioritising your own professional development over the client's needs and interests, potentially damaging the all-important trust on which the effectiveness of your relationship is founded. On the other hand, done well, this conversation can serve to strengthen your working relationship.

## A Conversation to Elicit Feedback

1 Explain the purpose of your request for feedback including what you will do with it and taking account of any confidentiality matters.
2 Ask clear, succinct, open questions. For example, questions starting with 'what' gives a person opportunities to open up about a topic whereas closed questions, eliciting 'Yes/No' answers are likely to shut the conversation down. Ask follow-up open questions to delve into the detail.
3 Listen with the intention of understanding, not to respond. Avoid being defensive and justifying a position.
4 Be prepared for potentially uncomfortable moments. You may be told things you would rather not hear, but you will learn from the experience.
5 Demonstrate you care about the answers. For example, give time and space for them to be explored together.
6 Hear and take on board the positive comments. It can be tempting to dwell on those areas that are problematic or could be improved, and take for granted something that is going well.
7 Finish by asking if there is anything else the person wants to add. Thank them for their time and contribution.

It is also important to consider the extent to which your client felt engaged with the process and what helped or hindered that engagement. For example, how effective were you in creating a safe space for your client taking account of their gender, self-identification, ethnic background, age, sexual orientation, disability and other personal circumstances that impact building and sustaining an appropriate and effective working relationship?

## The Client's Context

Another emphasis we are continually underlining in this book is the importance of taking account of the client's context and circumstances, both in your professional actions as well as in relation to your Effective Reflective Practice plan. Your client is part of a system, aspects of which they may be able to influence to a greater or lesser degree. The wider system will set formal and informal parameters about what is allowable and feasible in the client's particular context. Therefore, it is vital that in your review and learning you notice and consider the contextual factors that are in play for your client and the extent to which they are able to control or influence those factors. There will be some systemic factors that are not amenable to control or influence and the client may have to accept that this is the way things are. This does not mean of course that, for example, unacceptable working conditions or poor behaviour from colleagues should go unchallenged.

So, to what extent did the contextual circumstances help or hinder the realisation of your intended outcome? What factors were, and remain relevant that are supporting or impeding your efforts? What insights and learning can you find in reflecting on how the positive factors can be amplified and the negative ones minimised?

## HOW MIGHT DIFFERENT LEARNING THEORIES HELP YOU TO STRENGTHEN YOUR APPROACH TO LEARNING?

Much has been written about how children and adults learn. Here we will consider four major areas of thinking and draw out their benefits for the reflective practitioner.

### Kolb's Learning Cycle

In Chapter 1 we outlined the four features of David Kolb's learning cycle (1984): learning through concrete experience (i.e. 'doing'); learning through reflective observation; learning through conceptualisation (i.e. forming theories and/or linking experience to existing theories); and learning through active experimentation. We emphasised Kolb's (1984) assertion that the best learning occurs when all four types of learning are involved. Peter Honey and Alan Mumford (1982) extended Kolb's work into a description of four associated learning styles or preferences (Table 6.1). These styles are not innate, can be learnt and developed, and an individual may have more than one major preference.

**Table 6.1** Honey and Mumford's learning styles

| Activist learners ... | Reflector learners ... |
|---|---|
| • tend to think as they act | • tend to think before they act |
| • engross themselves in the here and now | • like time to prepare a response |
| • are stimulated by variety and like new, challenging experiences | • need space to think things through and consider the possibilities |
| • enjoy starting things off | • are comfortable with taking time to come to decisions without the pressure to respond |
| • are enthusiastic to join in and benefit from collaborating with other people | • are likely to listen and observe before making a contribution in group settings |
| • like to get things done | • build in time to analyse and evaluate |

| Theorist learners ... | Pragmatist learners ... |
|---|---|
| • like concepts, models and frameworks, and exploring underlying assumptions, and connections<br>• tend to want to see the bigger picture<br>• need to feel intellectually challenged<br>• are methodical and want structure and clarity of purpose<br>• are logical and seek the rationales for decisions, proposals and actions<br>• enjoy being stretched by the complexities of a situation | • like to know that something has relevance for them<br>• seek practical, deployable outcomes<br>• seek role models who have credibility and acknowledged expertise<br>• are interested in approaches that work<br>• enjoy trying out new ideas and approaches<br>• need strong connections to the real world |

*Source*: *The Learning Styles Questionnaire* by Peter Honey and Alan Mumford (2006)

You may already have a good idea of which approaches to learning you prefer, perhaps from your formal educational experiences or your work-related training. Informally you may also have a strong sense of how you like to learn outside your professional setting, which may or may not be different to the preferences you display at work. It is worth considering why there might be differences. If you are unsure, or want to explore your learning preferences further, there are online questionnaires based on Honey and Mumford's work which can help you to determine how you like to learn.

In undertaking a review of your Effective Reflective Practice cycle, give some thought to how your learning preferences might impact your explorations and how you might use the four styles as different lenses through which to view what is emerging. For example, if you are primarily an activist learner you are likely to focus in on the new areas of insight emerging from your deliberations, and you may be keen to move on quickly to implementing these ideas. It can be helpful to stand back and take time to look for insights that might be less obvious but nonetheless important (using the reflector style). Equally, giving some time and space to questioning the assumptions you are making (theorist style) and giving yourself permission to focus on the detail of how you will take things forward (pragmatist style) will lead to additional insights.

If your dominant preference is the reflector style, you will want to ensure there is sufficient time available to explore and assimilate insights, and will not be keen to move quickly to a conclusion without careful consideration of all possibilities. Again, thinking about the other learning styles, you will benefit from identifying clearly what needs to be done and moving to action without necessarily having all the required information (activist style). You will add to the depth of your thinking about the ideal scenario by establishing a clear sense of purpose with an associated structure for making things happen (theorist style). You may also want to turn your attention from an initial consideration of the big picture to the level of detail needed to take practical steps forward (from the pragmatist perspective).

With a theorist preference you will want to question your assumptions and to be intellectually stretched in the process. You enjoy exploring concepts and models and will be keen to see these explorations provide you with a clear sense of purpose. Applying the rest of the learning cycle, you will benefit from thinking about the actions you might take that are not readily proven by the available evidence (the activist style). You might also place a more deliberate focus on the emotional elements which are integral to your actions and insights (a feature drawn from the reflector preference). Having first researched the theories or concepts that underpin and inform your thinking you might adopt a pragmatist mindset to move into focusing on the practical implications of your deliberations.

Finally, if your learning preference falls more into the pragmatist part of the cycle, you will be clear about the connections between your deliberations and their relevance to the realities of your professional activities. You will have enjoyed experimenting with approaches and will be keen to continue giving things a try. The other features of the learning cycle offer you more benefits for the reflective review you are undertaking. For example, adopting a theorist perspective will help to ground your perceptions in relevant concepts and models and will provide a stronger rationale for the practical actions you want to take. Seeking out the excitement of applying your ideas to create novel experiences for you will broaden your thinking (an activist characteristic). Further, getting into more detailed analysis of the situation you are exploring (from the reflector perspective) will help to strengthen the practical conclusions you reach.

## Chris Argyris's Concept of Double Loop Learning

Based on Kolb's work, Chris Argyris (1993) developed the concepts of single and double loop learning. Single loop learning closely mirrors the learning cycle of action, reflection, conceptualisation and testing. Argyris believed that this was not always sufficient for dealing with complex realities, seeing single loop learning as valuable but essentially focused on problem-solving (i.e. making improvements to the existing system without questioning the system itself). Double loop learning involves more than simply fixing a problem and moves into challenging the assumptions, values and beliefs that underpin how the system operates.

Put simply, single loop learning can be seen as resolving issues in order to achieve a particular outcome, or 'doing things right'. Double loop learning focuses on questioning and changing the veracity of the intended outcome, or 'doing the right things'.

Double loop learning is a valuable concept to deploy as part of your reflective review as it will extend your efforts beyond straightforward problem-solving and into challenging the assumptions and beliefs you hold about what you are wanting to achieve and how it can be realised.

## Bruner's Constructivist Theory of Learning

Jerome Bruner's ideas about learning and how it should be organised within educational systems emerged in the 1960s and remain relevant today (Bruner, 1960). The core principle behind Bruner's theory of learning is that learners should be encouraged and enabled to discover the connections and relationships between facts and concepts themselves, rather than be told what these are by someone else. The most effective learning therefore takes place in situations where learners can be autonomous and are free to become active in constructing their own learning. For Bruner this also involves the conditions for them to build a better understanding of *how* they learn. This accords with our own assertion about Effective Reflective Practice: the practitioner needs to find ways of understanding and assimilating insights about their practice. Academics, professional trainers and the professional bodies can obviously be helpful enablers and guides of good practice. Ultimately, however, as a reflective practitioner you need to come to your own conclusions about how your reflective insights improve your practice.

Bruner coined the concept of the 'spiral curriculum' for children's education, believing that the fundamental features of any subject could be learnt at any age. His spiral involves the learner engaging with the same subject matter again and again throughout their development, each time at a more advanced level further up the 'spiral'. We believe this is a helpful concept for the reflective practitioner who may revisit learning and insights about a specific topic at more and more advanced levels, deepening their understanding, knowledge and skill with each twist of the spiral.

### An Example from Counselling

One of the initial skills that counsellors are encouraged to develop is listening. This is a core skill in counselling, which is a facilitative activity designed to enable clients to do the thinking for themselves. In day-to-day conversations people do not always listen attentively. Perhaps their mind is busy thinking about how they are about to respond, focusing on what is being triggered by the other person's words or simply switched off through boredom. In order to act as a mirror for a client's thoughts and ideas, a counsellor needs to move from this default position to one which embodies *active* listening. So a trainee counsellor will learn to dial down their own inner voice and focus in on being attentive to the client's words.

(*Continued*)

Encountering the skill of listening a little later in their development, the counsellor will now add in paying attention to the client's facial expressions and body language as other informative and valuable ways of listening.

Further along the counsellor's development pathway they will learn how to play back to the client in their own words the essential elements of what they have said, demonstrating to the client that they have *truly* listened. When the counsellor next visits the skill of listening they will concentrate on displaying genuine empathy for the client's situation so as to engender an even more powerful sense of being understood.

Listening is such an essential professional skill that counsellors will continue to revisit their effectiveness in this area throughout their career and continuing development so that they are always reviewing and extending their capability.

Bruner describes three phases of learning:

1 *Enactive learning* – which is based on learning through action (note the similarity here with the activist learning style discussed earlier).
2 *Iconic learning* – involving the development and use of images (usually visual), which represent the learning in the learner's mind. When you are learning something new it can be easier to assimilate if it can be presented to you or reinforced through pictures and diagrams. Incidentally, other icons involved in learning can be related to touch, hearing or smell. Clearly, the impact of these other factors will depend on your preferences for different modes of learning.
3 *Symbolic learning* – where learning is understood and expressed through language and other symbolic possibilities such as mathematics, music and other forms of art.

In child development terms, Bruner sees these three phases as a hierarchy with children progressing at different ages from Phase 1 to 3. However, he also acknowledges that adults continue to utilise all three modes of learning, even though the third is predominant.

Effective Reflective Practice embodies Bruner's ideas because the professional is continually involved in activities that allow them to notice recurring patterns and revisit their thinking, feelings, assumptions and beliefs about their capabilities.

In addition, Bruner introduced the term 'scaffolding', which involves breaking down complex tasks into smaller, more manageable ones. Bruner's concept also emphasises the social nature of learning by including the involvement of a third party who provides a sounding board and supportive guidance for the emerging learning. This is why we believe having a conversation with a trusted colleague about the insights emerging from the review of your reflective practice will have a powerful impact on the learning you take from the process. No doubt you will be able to recognise the scaffolding approach from aspects of your initial professional education, and probably in your continuing formal development activities, where more experienced colleagues will have helped you assimilate concepts and practices into your approach.

## Myers-Briggs Type Indicator

Another way of raising awareness of your learning preferences is the Myers–Briggs Type Indicator (Rogers, 2007). This is a psychometric instrument that gives you an indication of how you approach life, including how you like to learn. It is in common use in work-related development programmes so you may have encountered it at some point in your career already and therefore know your 'type'. If not, there are free MBTI questionnaires available online which will give you the data you need to make a decision about your type.

MBTI is based on four dimensions which describe your preferences for where you get your energy; how you perceive the world; how you make decisions; and how you live your life (see Table 6.2). These four dimensions combine to create 16 distinct personality types. Clearly, we are all unique individuals and there are as many 'types' in the world as there are people. Nonetheless the theory behind MBTI suggests everyone exhibits intricate and sophisticated versions of one of the 16 types. Having a clearer sense of your type helps you to have a better understanding of how you approach reflective practice.

**Table 6.2** Understanding your MBTI type

| Where you get your energy | |
|---|---|
| Extraversion (E): In contact and conversation with other people | Introversion (I): Reflecting on your own |
| **How you perceive the world** | |
| Sensing (S): Based on tangible evidence | Intuition (N): Looking for intangible possibilities |
| **How you make decisions** | |
| Thinking (T): Based on objectivity | Feeling (F): Centring on relationships and personal values |
| **How you live your life** | |
| Judging (J): Being organised and decisive | Perceiving (P): Remaining flexible and adaptable |

Please note that the terminology used to name the dimensions has specific meaning within the MBTI concept, which differs from the everyday use of the words. As with all such instruments it is important to take care not to use them in ways that risk stereotyping yourself or other people.

The MBTI questionnaire produces data for you to consider about your type presented as four letters, one from each of the dimension pairs (e.g. ENTJ). In essence the theory behind MBTI suggests that you will either be one end of the dimension or the other, although there are more complex questionnaires that place an individual's responses in positions along each dimension more accurately. Each of the MBTI types has implications for how individuals prefer to learn.

## Implications for Learning – Some Examples

If you have an Extravert preference, you will want to learn through concrete activity and experience and most likely in collaboration with others. You will be drawn to projects, the learning that arises from practical experience and workshop-type contexts where you can participate.

As an Introvert learner you will seek opportunities for quiet reflection and independent learning, generally preferring learning situations where you can observe interactions and learn from others with more knowledge, such as demonstrations and lectures.

If you are a Sensing type, you will prefer concrete learning experiences, with a particular interest and focus on factual and verifiable information. You will seek clear pathways in a programme of learning so you can see the connections between the different parts.

If you have a preference for Intuition, you will prefer abstract and conceptual forms of learning. You will be interested in an academic approach with clear opportunities for you to direct your own learning.

As a Thinking type you will also have a preference for abstract and conceptual learning and outcomes that are practical, feasible and deliverable. You will be 'hands-on' and engage best with structured learning opportunities.

With a Feeling preference you will prefer concrete learning experiences with methodologies that embody holistic approaches, drawing on a range of potential sources. You will have a particular interest in the implications of the learning for people.

If you are a learner with a preference for Judging you will be keen to engage with abstract and conceptual learning activities. You will thrive where there is a clear plan for the learning, perhaps delivered with a more didactic approach as well as opportunities for self-study.

As a Perceiving type you will prefer learning opportunities that allow your natural curiosity the space to keep open how the learning evolves. You will seek concrete learning experiences with frequent chances to experiment.

Clearly the different dimensions intersect in important ways to create more complex learning environment requirements for individual learners. As with the learning styles material presented earlier, it is beneficial to have a clear understanding of your preferences and how they are likely to impact your approach to learning and reflective practice. This understanding will help you reflect on your practice in ways that make you feel comfortable. In addition, we are encouraging you to step outside your comfort zone to look at your reflective practice activity from other, less familiar perspectives because this will produce other insights that you might otherwise miss.

## The VARK Learning Styles

Another helpful way to consider your learning preferences is offered by the VARK framework. This approach proposes that there are four distinctly different types of learners:

1 Visual learners focus on what they can see. They learn from visual representations, such as illustrations, graphics, diagrams, flowcharts and maps. They benefit from the visual presentation of connections and patterns, and colour will be important. They have a tendency to create their own visual representations of information through, for example, doodling and mindmaps.
2 Auditory learners learn by taking in information they hear. They also benefit from reciting new information and reading aloud as well as opportunities to talk, including discussing questions with others. They will be interested in audio presentations of information and podcasts. They have a tendency to work out their ideas while speaking, rather than thinking them through in advance.
3 Reading and writing learners prefer to write things down and often make copious notes. They have a strong interest in the written word and are drawn to books, articles, journals and other text-based material. Their own writing will form an integral part of how they go about understanding things, often helping them to take things apart before making sense of them through reconstruction.
4 Kinaesthetic learners are tactile learners and learn best by doing and a 'hands-on' approach. They have a tendency to learn through relating new information to their own personal experience. Their preference for acting out or role-playing, involves them in bringing all of their senses into the process, including touch. Being energetic, moving around is likely to help the learning to happen.

In Chapter 9, we explore a diverse range of creative methods for reflective practice. The VARK framework can be helpful as an indicator of the types of creative activity with which you will want to engage. For example, if you are a visual learner you will be drawn to the visual approaches we have outlined. Auditory learners are likely to find, for example, writing poetry and reading it aloud (if only to yourself) productive. If your preference is for the reading and writing style, journaling and different ways of writing down and organising your thoughts will be attractive. Finally, readers who are kinaesthetic will find tactile methods, which are based on touch and movement, beneficial.

### Making Use of the Learning Theories

In reality you will have not just one learning style but a range of preferences and you will likely deploy different styles in different circumstances. Underpinning all these learning theories is the notion that the best learning occurs when you mobilise your preferences *and* when a number of them are in play together. In their learning cycle, for instance, Kolb (1984) emphasises the importance of seeing the four styles as complementary, each adding something different and valuable to the learning process. It can be helpful to see the cycle as a guide, working your way around it and viewing a topic from each of the lenses in turn.

We therefore encourage you to become aware of your learning preferences, to make intentional use of those preferences in your reflective practice and also to step outside your learning comfort zones regularly to gain the benefits of different perspectives.

### Neurodiversity

Taking account of your neurotype will be an important consideration. If you are neurodivergent, you may come at your learning in ways that are not neurotypical. For example, some neurodivergent learners need to assimilate new learning in bite-sized chunks with clear sequential steps. Others may require frequent periods of 'downtime' to re-energise themselves. Clearly, there are many types of neurodivergence and there is no one-size-fits-all approach. As for all learners, gaining clarity about, and testing out, how best you learn will provide a firm foundation for your ongoing development.

## HOW TO CAPTURE YOUR THOUGHTS AND INSIGHTS

One of the most commonly used ways of capturing your learning is through journaling. Research studies suggest that journaling reduces stress and anxiety, helps you learn more effectively from your experiences, improves communication skills and memory, boosts self-belief and self-esteem, improves your mood, helps with problem-solving, builds your creativity and helps you deal with challenging or traumatic experiences.

Journaling can take many forms: hand-written notebooks, e-documents on a laptop, voice notes on a smartphone, emails to yourself, video recordings, and art and nature journals. If your preference is for using technology, there are a number of software packages and apps online that are specifically designed for journaling purposes. While the use of modern technology has obvious benefits, for example, ease of use and password-protected security, many commentators encourage the use of hand-writing as a way of deliberately slowing down the process of journaling to allow for greater reflection in the moment. Ultimately it will be for you to experiment and find out what you enjoy and what works for you in your professional context.

The most important aspect of successful journaling is establishing and maintaining a regular habit. Again, you need to work out what time intervals and scheduling work best for you. Do you find it easier to journal first thing in the morning before the day gets underway, or last thing in the evening as a way of wrapping up how the day has gone? In this book we are focused on Effective Reflective Practice about professional matters. You might therefore prefer to journal after each professional encounter with a client, or at a time as close to those interactions as is possible. The length of time you spend is up to you. Deciding on an amount of time and sticking to that for each journaling session can be helpful in sustaining the habit.

It is important to remember that your journal is a private record of your thoughts, and anything goes. It is likely to be a messy and organic process, at least in its initial creation until you have had the time to reflect in more detail on what is emerging from your writing. It is a good idea to separate the tasks of capturing your initial thoughts and editing those thoughts in order to crystallise your reflections into insights. One way to keep to the journaling habit is to commit to pairing with a colleague to share your insights and learning on a regular basis.

While your journaling will concentrate on the intended outcome you have established for yourself in your reflective practice plan, it can also be beneficial to journal on a regular basis about your practice more broadly. In any case, you are likely to find that these wider reflections will feed into and inform your thinking about the more specific outcomes. Your journal can also be a place to capture quotes, observations and ideas from sources completely unrelated to your professional activities, such as literature, art, music and films that have triggered some insights about your work. Words may not always be the most effective way to express your thoughts and emotions so be open to using symbols, diagrams, doodles and sketches in your journal.

Finally, as we are emphasising throughout this book, include notes and reflections in your journal about the assumptions you are making about people and situations, and the wider, systemic factors in the organisational context.

Maintaining a journaling habit takes commitment and motivation. It can be useful to always have your journal to hand, so you can readily record thoughts and ideas whenever they arise. If you find yourself beginning to see regular journaling as a chore, try mixing things up a bit by, for example, changing the time of day, journaling in a different environment or intentionally focusing your writing on what you are grateful for in relation to your current professional practice. Gratitude journaling is recommended by positive psychologists as an effective way to remain appreciative and boost your wellbeing. On the occasions when you are stuck for what to write, return to your intended outcome for your reflective practice and use this as a starting point for journaling. Alternatively, free-form writing from an introductory phrase, such as 'When I'm working at my best I …', can help you to break through blockages. Free-form writing involves keeping your pen moving across the page for a set amount of time, writing down whatever comes to mind and ignoring any grammatical and spelling mistakes as you go just to see what emerges.

If you are engaged in reflective practice in order to gain a qualification or further professional credentialing, maintaining a reflective journal as a regular habit will provide you with a rich source of information from which to write an assignment or provide the relevant evidence required by your professional body. In the next chapter, we will use journaling as a starting point for writing formally to demonstrate your ability to reflect in an appropriate way for your professional field.

## SUMMARY

In this chapter, we have recommended that it is helpful to know your preferred ways of learning. This allows you to play to your strengths. At the same time, new insights can emerge from adopting learning approaches that are less familiar to you. We have also highlighted the value of journaling and capturing your learning as you work through the Effective Reflective Practice process. In the next chapter, we will present a template for providing evidence of undertaking Effective Reflective Practice.

### Find Out More

Argyris, C. (1993). *Knowledge for Action: A Guide to Overcoming Barriers to Organizational Change*. San Francisco, CA: Jossey Bass.

Bruner, J. S. (1960). *The Process of Education*. Cambridge, MA: Harvard University Press.

Honey, P. & Mumford, A. (2006). *The Learning Styles Questionnaire, 80-item version*. Maidenhead: Peter Honey.

Kolb, D. A. (1984). *Experiential Learning: Experience as the Source of Learning and Development*. Englewood Cliffs, NJ: Prentice-Hall.

Rogers, J. (2007). *Sixteen Personality Types – At Work in Organisations*. London: Management Futures Ltd.

# 7

# HOW TO WRITE FOR ASSESSMENT

This chapter will cover:

- A recommended template for reflective writing
- Practical suggestions for reflective writing
  - How to show you have engaged in Effective Reflective Practice
  - How to write up a cycle of Effective Reflective Practice
- An overview of the process for submitting a piece of reflective writing

Now that you have completed your cycle of Effective Reflective Practice, it is time to write it up for formal presentation as part of a qualification programme or a professional credentialing process. You will be using the thoughts, feelings and insights you have captured in your journal throughout the cycle. These might be in a raw and unedited form and are likely to lead to further questions to explore. By the time you turn your attention to writing up your cycle of Effective Reflective Practice, it is likely that your journal will be full of notes, observations, insights, doodles, sketches, diagrams and tables. Not everything in your journal will be appropriate to use as part of the write-up. Having said that, capturing the essence of what you have learnt is a critically important part of the Effective Reflective Practice process. Remember, one of its purposes is to bring about positive change for your clients and yourself; the other is to grow and develop. There is invaluable learning in noticing and recording as you progress through your reflective practice cycle. Emergent thoughts, feelings and questions are part of the evolution of your thinking and your professional practice.

As it will be a formal written document, it is vital to follow key examination guidance. This is an often cited piece of advice: read and understand the question. In this case, the first step is to ensure that you are certain about what is being asked of you. When you read the instructions to the assignment or assessment, make sure to focus particularly on the *depth* and *proportion* of reflection that is expected of you. Pay attention to the word count and use the template presented below unless another format is specified.

As educators and assessors of reflective writing ourselves, we know that a common error is for students and practitioners to dedicate too much of the limited word count to describing the facts of a situation, rather than focusing on the impact of those facts on their thoughts, feelings, behaviour and practice. Remember that you are being assessed on how you reflect and learn. Assessors are more interested in your reflections, insights and learning, and how you intend to apply that learning than a blow-by-blow description of what you did. 'Wasting' valuable words setting out the details of what happened will reduce the words available for you to demonstrate your ability to reflect, explain what you have learnt and show how all of this has led to improvements in your practice.

## RECOMMENDED TEMPLATE FOR REFLECTIVE WRITING

**Figure 7.1** Effective Reflective Practice framework

**Table 7.1** Effective Reflective Practice cycle

<table>
<tr><td>Effective Reflective Practice cycle</td><td>[insert the focus of reflective practice]</td></tr>
<tr><td>Practitioner</td><td>[insert your name and student number (if appropriate) here]</td></tr>
<tr><td>Date</td><td>[insert date of completing this review]</td></tr>
<tr><td colspan="2">Part 1: Brief background and context [20% of word count]</td></tr>
<tr><td colspan="2">Intention<br>This section should answer the question: What was behind your decision to work on enhancing an aspect of your professional practice?<br>To include:<br>• Motivations<br>• Values and principles<br>• Professional aspirations.</td></tr>
<tr><td colspan="2">Outcome<br>This section should be very brief and explicit.<br>To include:<br>• An explicit measurable outcome<br>• An explanation of how you will know that the outcome has been achieved<br>• Indicators of a successful outcome.</td></tr>
<tr><td colspan="2">Plan<br>Provide a very brief outline of what you intended using the format presented below.<br>The plan should be followed by a short paragraph relating to ethics and equalities:<br>• Explain that you undertook an ethical review of your plan and provide an example of an ethical question relevant to this reflective practice cycle.<br>• Explain that you did an Equality Impact Assessment and provide an example of something that required adaptation following the assessment.<br>End this section with your hypothesis or hypotheses:<br>• Present these clearly in bullet point format.</td></tr>
<tr><td colspan="2">Experimentation<br>Share the results of the experiments:<br>• Highlight what worked well in the experiment<br>• Highlight what did not work in the experiment<br>• End this section by concluding whether your hypotheses were proven or disproven<br>• Present these as bullet points by repeating the hypothesis or hypotheses followed by whether they were proven or disproven.</td></tr>
<tr><td colspan="2">Part 2: Reflections and learning [80% of word count]</td></tr>
<tr><td colspan="2">Provide a brief appraisal of the reflective practice cycle.<br>[Write out in a paragraph]<br>1 Was the desired outcome achieved for the client?<br>2 Did you achieve your initial intention?<br>3 What did you learn about yourself and your practice?</td></tr>
</table>

*(Continued)*

**Table 7.1** (Continued)

| |
|---|
| 4 If you achieved the outcomes, to what extent do they align with your original intention?<br>Based on your review, identify the insights and learning that emerged for you. |
| **Your motivation**<br>[Write out in a paragraph]<br>• How motivational was your original positive intention?<br>• What did you learn about yourself in setting your intention? (e.g. how closely aligned was your intention with your purpose and values?)<br>• How did your strengths and learning preferences support your motivation? |
| **Your outcome**<br>[Write out in a paragraph]<br>• What are your reflections on the outcomes you chose? |
| **Your plan**<br>[Write out in a paragraph]<br>• What worked well?<br>• What did you learn about your strengths?<br>• Were there any parts of the plan that turned out to be less useful?<br>• How good were you at sticking to your plan?<br>• What ethical issues emerged and how did you deal with them?<br>• What changes did you implement following the Equality Impact Assessment? |
| **Your experiments**<br>[Write out in a paragraph]<br>• What was the most important learning you took away from the experimentation phase?<br>• What did you learn about yourself, your clients and the wider context as you experimented?<br>• What aspects of your experiment worked particularly well?<br>• What elements could have benefitted from further revision?<br>• To what extent did stepping outside your comfort zones (e.g. in terms of learning preferences and strengths) help? |
| **Your conclusion**<br>[Write out in a paragraph]<br>• What did you learn about your impact on clients and others?<br>• In what specific ways will you make improvements to your practice?<br>• How will you test that these improvements are benefitting clients?<br>• Overall, what did you learn about yourself as a professional that might have applications more broadly in your life? |
| **References**<br>[Where you draw on other people's work, such as books, articles and research papers, it is courteous and proper to include a reference to that work. This should detail their name, the full title of the work, the publisher and the date of publication. If your reflective piece is part of a qualification programme or credentialing, references are essential to demonstrate your engagement with existing practices and relevant theories.]<br>• Include 3–6 references using APA (American Psychological Association) style. |

*Note:* Two worked examples of the plan are included in Appendix 1 on pp. 131-146.

## PRACTICAL SUGGESTIONS FOR REFLECTIVE WRITING

When writing up your Effective Reflective Practice for the purposes of assessment or accreditation, it is necessary to demonstrate your ability to reflect on your practice in a way that generates learning and leads to a change in your practice. To put it simply, your reflective writing should (1) demonstrate that you have engaged with the Effective Reflective Practice process and (2) that this had led to learning, insights and a change in professional practice. While it is expected that the content should be introspective and personal, when submitting for assessment to an educational institution or professional body, your reflective writing must follow certain academic conventions. In the section below, we will set out clearly what is expected.

### How to Show That You Have Engaged in a Cycle of Effective Reflective Practice

The primary requirement will be to demonstrate that you have worked through a complete cycle of reflective practice. For best results, select an area of professional practice which is meaningful to you. This will make the task more engaging. If you have followed the Effective Reflective Practice process, it will then be relatively straightforward to review your notes and undertake the following:

- Set out the context for your desire to improve your practice
- Explain your positive intention
- State your desired outcomes
- Explain what your clients would experience if you were successful
- Briefly present the plan that you initially developed
- Consider the ethical implications of your plan
- Provide some snapshots of the experimentation stage
- Reflect on the extent to which the cycle was effective
- Capture all the insights and learning that emerged from the process
- Highlight what is different about your professional practice.

The points above demonstrate that you have been through a complete cycle of Effective Reflective Practice. In addition, you should follow an academic writing style that will provide evidence of careful reflection and critical thinking.

### How To Write It Up

#### Adopt An Academic Writing Style

If your reflective writing is being used for the purposes of academic or professional assessment, it is important that the writing follows academic conventions. This is so the work can be assessed fairly in relation to other submissions. By asking everyone to follow the same rules, it is easier for your assessors to make academic and professional judgements about whether you have met the required expectations. Academic convention also requires you to acknowledge people when you share their ideas or theories.

## Write in the First Person

For reflective writing, it is acceptable and expected that you use the first person when writing up your insights and learning. You should use 'I', 'me' or 'we' throughout your assignment. The reason for this is that this assignment centres on your *personal* reflections and it is important for your assessor to understand *your* experience of the process.

## Explore Ideas in Depth

Reflective practice should lead to deeper thinking and exploration of your professional activities. Therefore, your reflective writing should move beyond surface-level thinking and description. Frequent exploration of your thoughts, emotions and new insights will demonstrate that you are thinking deeply about your practice. You are trying to convey a sense of professional curiosity.

## Reference Relevant Theories and/or Research

While the purpose of your reflective writing is to explore your own thoughts and emotions, academic convention requires you to consider your professional practice in relation to existing theories or research. When you position your current or future practices alongside relevant academic theories or recent research, it shows that you are curious and open to learning. This provides your assessor with evidence of your ability to engage in critical thinking. The theories or research studies could be the starting point for your reflection, they could inform your plan of action, or they can be used to understand the success or otherwise of your reflective practice.

### Practical Tips

Below are some practical tips that will demonstrate that you are engaging fully with the Effective Reflective Practice process. These have been generated through discussions with students, professionals and academics who have written or assessed pieces of reflective writing.

1 Write up your assignment by working through the Effective Reflective Practice cycle step-by-step. This will result in a clear structure that is logical and easy to follow. For examples of this, see the completed templates (Appendix 1).

2 Include commentary about your strengths as well as areas for development. This demonstrates self-awareness. For example, 'I know that I can be very persistent when I consider something to be important. This can help me to stick with things through difficult times. But I need to take into account that I have had feedback that this can come across as stubbornness to colleagues and friends.'
3 Admit to being wrong at some points in your narrative or include examples of mistakes or errors that you made. This shows that you are being honest and authentic in your writing. For example, 'When I started this process, I made some assumptions about how my colleagues would react to my proposals. With hindsight, I should have talked to colleagues beforehand. Many of them were much more supportive than I had expected.'
4 Use rhetorical questions and tentative language. This demonstrates that you are curious and committed to learning and professional growth. One example is, 'I wonder if I should have given people more time to come round to the realities of the situation?' Another example is, 'As far as I can tell, the new initiatives were welcomed by my colleagues. People seemed, on the whole, to relish the opportunity to try new things.'
5 Highlight new learning and insights. Be explicit about what you learnt and any insights that emerged, especially during the experimentation stage. When presenting insights, explain how the new learning might impact on your professional practice. For example, 'It became clear to me through my experimentation that taking more time before responding to irritating emails would allow me to communicate better. Building in some "downtime" before answering such emails is likely to have positive impacts on my relationships, but also on my own wellbeing!'
6 Avoid the temptation to say that the reflective practice cycle has confirmed what you knew all along. This would be evidence that there has been no new learning. For example, 'Having been through a cycle of Effective Reflective Practice, I am now even more convinced that my style of leadership is what this organisation needs at this time.'
7 Include statements that recognise the complexity of people, situations and contexts. This shows that you are engaging in critical thinking and avoiding the trap of looking for 'silver bullet' solutions. For example, 'While the new way that I welcome clients into my office seems to be having a positive impact, I need to continually evaluate its effectiveness, especially taking into account personal preferences and cultural considerations.'
8 Minimise descriptive text and include more analysis. This demonstrates that you are being critical in your reflections. For example, there is no need to explain a new process that you are introducing in great detail. Rather,

(*Continued*)

provide a summary of the change and focus your narrative on the possible benefits of the change.

9 Make sure to include commentary about your emotions alongside your thoughts. This shows that you are going deeper in the exploration of your reactions. For example, 'I have often wondered whether I should be seeing some of these patients personally before their operations - and whether that would make a significant difference to their experience. Even as I reflect on this, I notice that I have a feeling of slight unease or anxiety.'

10 Comment on how your behaviours and professional practice relate to your personal values. This shows that you are aware of your principles and deeply-held beliefs. For example, 'I do find the final sessions with my clients very difficult. One of my beliefs is that I should always finish what I start. So the final session can make me feel very uncomfortable, especially when I think that there is more that we could have achieved together.'

## AN OVERVIEW OF THE COMPLETE PROCESS FOR SUBMITTING A PIECE OF REFLECTIVE WRITING

1 Re-read the first seven chapters of this book.
2 Undertake a complete cycle of Effective Reflective Practice, using a real example from your professional context.
3 Use this book as a reference and guide throughout the cycle.
4 Keep a detailed reflective journal to make notes and capture your learning as you work through the cycle.
5 Read the assignment guidelines of your academic institution or professional body carefully.
6 Refer to this chapter as you draft your piece of reflective writing.
7 Use the template provided unless a different one is recommended by your assessors.
8 Once your first draft is complete, refer to the Reflective Writing Marking Guide (available on the Sage website https://study.sagepub.com/nieuwerburghlove1e and in worked examples in Appendix 2) to compare your assignment to the academic expectations. It may be helpful to ask a friend or colleague to read your assignment and assess it using the Reflective Writing Marking Guide.
9 Make any necessary changes or edits and read through the entire document one last time.
10 Submit your assignment.

## SUMMARY

Essentially, when writing up the reflective practice cycle, you are minimising the *descriptive* component. The first part of the write-up provides a *brief* explanation of your intention, your desired outcome, the plan that you developed, the result of your experiment and whether you were able to bring about positive change. The second part is the heart of the write-up. This is where you should put most of your effort, explaining what you have learnt through the cycle. In this chapter, we have provided you with a template and practical ideas and suggestions for completing and submitting a piece of reflective writing.

### Find Out More

Moon, J. (1999). *Reflection in Learning and Professional Development*. London: Kogan Page.

See Appendix 1 for two examples of reflective write-ups for assessment purposes. The examples are accompanied by a marksheet providing an indicative assessment against our suggested Marking Guide. You will find this in Appendix 2.

# 8

# HOW TO MAKE IT HAPPEN IN ORGANISATIONS

This chapter will cover:

- The importance of reflective practice in organisations and systems
- Leading through reflective practice and for reflective practice
- Creating a climate for Effective Reflective Practice
- Deciding topics to bring to a collaborative reflective practice conversation
- Managing and facilitating the conversation

From the outset, our intention (as authors) has been to promote the effective use of reflective practice by professionals in ways that have a positive impact on clients and stakeholders. An important premise is that this work should have positive wellbeing outcomes for the professional as well. To go one level deeper, we hope to support you, our readers, to thrive so that you can be of better service to the people you serve. Necessarily, we started this writing project with a sharp focus on you, the reader. Our first concern was what *you* need for *you* to be at your best, as a learner, as a professional and as a person. The Effective Reflective Practice framework presented in this book directs attention to your clients and stakeholders. Reflective practice is not effective unless there is a positive impact on them.

We want to be transparent. We do have an agenda. That is to share a practice that has been transformational for us, as professional coaches. Through this type of reflective practice, we believe that we have been able to deliver high-quality support to our clients. Through our own practice and our professional learning, we have come to understand the centrality of reflective practice in helping us to be better aligned with our values and principles. While other models of reflective practice exist, we are committed to promoting the model presented in this book – *Effective* Reflective Practice – because it integrates wellbeing into the process. We believe that professionals require and deserve time to invest in their own wellbeing and development.

From the outset, we defined some foundational principles that underpin Effective Reflective Practice. The first of these was that there can be no learning or self-development without self-awareness. We hope that your self-awareness has been sharpened whilst engaging with the ideas presented in this book. We also identified systemic awareness as necessary for Effective Reflective Practice. In other words, you need to have self-awareness whilst also being aware of the context you are in. The second principle was that reflective practice will be more effective when the professional is open-minded and curious. Third, we emphasised the importance of intentionality, arguing that professionals should be clear about their positive intentions for the future. The final principle was that reflective practice will be good for professionals and their wellbeing if they can be compassionate to themselves and others as they do the important work that they do.

Up to this point, we have been focusing on you, the reader, and a process that you can adopt to engage in and demonstrate reflective practice. In this chapter, we broaden the scope of our exploration, considering the best ways of creating contexts that are conducive to the foundational principles discussed above. What can we do to promote Effective Reflective Practice within organisations?

## THE IMPORTANCE OF REFLECTIVE PRACTICE IN ORGANISATIONS AND SYSTEMS

In some professions, such as coaching and counselling, reflective practice is achieved through supervision, which is an accepted part of the continuing professional development of practitioners. To different degrees, supervision is built into the ongoing credentialing processes of the relevant professional bodies. Supervision is essentially reflective practice about a practitioner's work undertaken with another, usually more experienced, colleague. Sometimes the supervising colleague is a more senior member of an organisation perhaps with line management authority over the person being supervised. The term 'supervision' can be problematic as it implies an unequal power relationship, but best practice involves practitioners meeting in supervision as professional equals. They develop and maintain a collaborative partnership with a focus on enabling the person being supervised to deeply explore aspects of their practice in order to draw out the learning and ways to strengthen their capabilities for working with clients.

A starting point for a supervision conversation is often a specific experience with a particular client. The most effective supervisory practice will enable the practitioner to discover the wider implications for how they work with all clients and will include detailed consideration of the contexts those clients are working in and how these impact ways of working and relating with others.

One framework places a clear emphasis on the wellbeing of the practitioner by focusing on the restorative function of supervision (Proctor, 2008) as one way of being able to express and explore their doubts, concerns and fears about their practice. This function works alongside two other key purposes of supervision, which focus on the attainment of accepted professional standards, including ethics, and the overall development of the practitioner.

Whatever framework is used in different professional contexts, supervision has three essential purposes:

1 support for, and development of, the professional in the service of high-quality work
2 ensuring the wellbeing of clients is at the forefront of the professional's activities
3 protecting the integrity and reputation of the organisation the professional is working for (either as an employee or a contractor) and the profession itself.

Supervision can happen one-to-one, in groups and between peers who bring their different perspectives to enable each other to unpack the detail of how they work.

## LEADING THROUGH REFLECTIVE PRACTICE AND FOR REFLECTIVE PRACTICE

Leaders have an obligation to encourage and nurture reflective practice among their professional colleagues. For our purposes, we are defining leaders as anyone with responsibility for the performance and development of others. In addition to those people with formal managerial responsibilities a leader can also be, for example, a project manager or an expert in a specialist field who needs to engage with others to get things done. Creating a climate where reflective practice is the accepted norm starts with the leader themselves. As an individual, their own reflective practice habit will inform how they operate in their particular professional field and will also influence how they lead and manage others, how they control and influence vital factors in the organisation and indeed the wider system of which that organisation is a part. So, Effective Reflective Practice is an essential part of a leader's personal professional development and, given their role, will have important impacts on the development and performance of others as well as the wider achievements of their organisation.

Creating a climate that fosters reflective practice for all starts with a degree of openness about their own reflective habit so that the leader is acting intentionally as a role model. Adopting some of the ideas outlined later in this chapter, the leader can establish and maintain the appropriate conditions in their professional and organisational context to facilitate others' reflective practice routines. This will require the leader to be transparent about how they go about reflecting on their practice and the benefits that result. It will also require openness about 'mistakes' and 'failure', or areas that require improvement to encourage others to be honest about things that may be holding them and the organisation back. As we have emphasised throughout this book, the ultimate focus is on the client and their outcomes. There may, of course, be other 'clients' involved in the chain of activities that takes place before a product or service is finally delivered. These will be other colleagues in the organisation who rely on the work of the leader and their team in order to make their own contribution. It can be helpful to ask the question: Who in the organisation makes up the deficit when our work does not come up to scratch?

In designing and implementing a process for Effective Reflective Practice, a leader will take into account:

- their particular professional context: What are the formal requirements for reflective practice and continuing professional development in this area? What additional ways of working need to be in place for reflective practice to flourish in this setting?
- the diversity of the team they lead: How will the different kinds and levels of expertise be accommodated? How will the difference of perspectives and ways of working associated, for example, with gender, ethnicity and neurodiversity be celebrated and mobilised in the service of the collective good? Leaders often find that creating the conditions for people to explore these kinds of questions and shape the answers works better than making assumptions about others and what they might, or might not, bring to the table.

In addition to role-modelling by leaders in an organisation, what else can be done to create an environment that welcomes and encourages Effective Reflective Practice? The following conditions will be most conducive:

- policies that demonstrate that the organisation respects its people
- professional trust (through giving staff autonomy to carry out their roles)
- performance review that focuses on outcomes (rather than input)
- clarity of organisational objectives with emphasis on outcomes for stakeholders
- high positive expectations of professionalism
- time and space allocated for reflective practice and professional learning
- skill development to support one's own and other people's reflective practice.

## CREATING A CLIMATE FOR EFFECTIVE REFLECTIVE PRACTICE

Throughout this book we have highlighted the benefits to be gained from Effective Reflective Practice that involves conversations with others. If you work in a field that has well-established processes for supervision as outlined above, you will be involved in collaborative activities designed to deepen your reflective practice and we encourage you to take full advantage of the opportunities open to you. If you work in a professional field where such activities are not part of the fabric of your practice. we encourage you to find ways that work for you and colleagues where you can share the findings of your own individual reflective practice and help each other to go deeper with the insights and learning. The simplest way to do this is to 'buddy up' with someone you trust and set aside regular times to meet and explore your practice. In this section we outline some practical ideas for how you can provide some structure for your conversations. We suggest you use and adapt this process for your own purposes.

Essentially you are creating an environment characterised by trust where you can safely and confidentially explore aspects of your practice that may at times prove challenging to open up about. It is essential to agree a set of ground rules for how you will work together. These are likely to include answers to the questions in the box below.

### How will we Ensure People Feel Safe?

- How will we ensure confidentiality - both for ourselves and for the clients whose circumstances we will be bringing into the room?
- What needs to happen for each of us to feel safe to bring up sensitive topics or to reveal aspects of ourselves or our practice that we feel embarrassed or ashamed about?
- How will we ensure we can explore with each other without being judged or criticised?

### What is the Right Balance between Support and Constructive Challenge?

- What levels and balance of support and constructive challenge are we seeking for each other?
- How will we make sure our wellbeing is at the heart of our conversations and that we work together with respect and compassion?
- How will we signal that we need time out for further personal reflection, or to reorientate ourselves to the task in hand, particularly after a challenging moment?

### How will we Ensure Everyone has a Voice that is Heard?

- How will we celebrate the many differences between us, maximising what we can gain from our different characteristics, backgrounds and experiences?

*(Continued)*

- How will we ensure that our similarities do not lead us to make unquestioned assumptions about where our reflections are taking us?
- How will we make sure we pay attention to our feelings and emotions as well as our thoughts and behaviours?

### How will we take into Account the Context and Systemic Factors?

- What support or conditions do we need to put in place to enable each of us to be able to contribute to, and gain from, the conversation?
- What will we do if issues emerge that have wider ethical ramifications and which require an active response beyond the conversation?
- How might important and useful observations about broader systemic factors be communicated to the relevant people without breaching any confidences?

## DECIDING TOPICS TO BRING TO A COLLABORATIVE REFLECTIVE PRACTICE CONVERSATION

The agenda of this kind of conversation is in your hands. It is likely it will have emerged from your own individual reflective practice and exploring the topic with a colleague will deepen your understanding and learning. Alternatively, it can also be helpful to see what comes to mind in the moment, rather than preparing something in detail in advance.

You can bring any topic related to your practice that you wish to explore. A common misunderstanding is that the conversation should only focus on problems in your work or areas of difficulty. We, the authors, are both supervisors of coaches, and in our supervisory work are at pains to stress that coaches should not turn up to our sessions saying 'I've had no problems with my coaching, so I have nothing to bring to supervision.' These sessions are opportunities for development and improvement and as a result there should *always* be something to explore. Of course, it may indeed be a problem, and it may also be:

- a success you have had in your work that you wish to explore to discover the causes of that success
- preparation for an upcoming meeting with a client
- exploration of an issue or challenge you have not yet experienced but you anticipate might be sensitive for you
- a particular area of your practice that you wish to strengthen or a new skill you wish to acquire.

### Deciding Group Size

Collaborative reflective practice can take place very effectively in pairs or in small groups. Working in pairs has the advantage of allowing more time for each professional and a more intimate setting for the conversation, which can create opportunities to go deeper. It can be easier to establish trust and safety because there is only one other person involved. Small groups on the other hand offer a wider range of contributions and perspectives, which adds to the potential for learning and can be more economical in the use of time where this is at a premium. We recommend a maximum group size of four to give everyone sufficient time for their reflections.

## MANAGING AND FACILITATING THE CONVERSATION

Whatever you have decided about group size it will be important to manage the conversation so that everyone involved has an equal amount of time. It can be easy for time to run away with itself because, for example, interest in what the first person brings overwhelms the conversation. One way to make the best use of time is to encourage participants to minimise how much factual information they provide about a particular situation. It is helpful to allocate the role of timekeeper to one member of the group. Beyond the need for a minimal amount of information to enable others to make sense of the situation the background facts are not the most important aspect of the collaborative reflective activity. Far more important are the emotions and insights that have been surfaced as a result of individual reflections about the situation. You may be surprised to discover how few facts about a situation you really need to understand in order for a very productive reflective discussion to take place.

Use the Effective Reflective Practice framework to structure the conversation with each participant focusing in on those parts of the process that proved the most productive in terms of their original intention. Again, it will not be necessary to lay out all the detail, rather a clear focus on the most powerful moments will suffice. In each person's time slot keep the focus on that individual and their reflections. Adopt a collaborative approach where you ask open questions to help them reflect in the moment on what they are presenting. At the end of their time, encourage them to briefly outline what they have gained from the conversation. These may be action points they have decided for themselves. However, be aware that the purpose of the conversation is for people to deepen their learning and gain insights about their practice rather than to ensure that everyone leaves the room with a clear action plan. While the emerging insights may naturally lead to the crystallisation of some actions, the absence of action points does not indicate that the conversation has 'failed'. Enhanced self-awareness is a positive outcome and it may be that further individual reflection later stimulates appropriate related actions.

We have continually emphasised that Effective Reflective Practice is about exploring individual professional activity in an organisational, and wider systemic, context. In the fields of coaching and counselling a very effective way to turn the focus of reflective attention to the systemic factors involves the use of Peter Hawkins and Nick Smith's 'Seven-Eyed' supervision model (2013). The 'seven eyes' provide for seven different perspectives on the relationship between an individual professional and their client:

1 How the client shows up
2 The professional's interventions
3 How the professional shows up
4 The relationship between the professional and the client
5 The relationship between the supervisor and the professional
6 What the supervisor experiences
7 The wider system within which the client (and the professional) are operating.

This is a framework designed for use in coaching and counselling supervision. However, it alerts all reflective practitioners to the importance of exploring how the wider system impacts what goes on between a professional and their client. The seventh eye focuses on the wider context and invites exploration of:

- the broader factors in a client's life that are influencing their thoughts, emotions and behaviours
- the team dynamics of which the professional is a part
- the relationships between the team and other relevant teams in the organisation
- the impact of the relationships the organisation has with other organisations which play a part in enabling the work with clients
- any regulating bodies involved in the professional's field, including established ethical frameworks and standards
- factors in the professional's life beyond work that affect their pratice.

From this brief list you can see that there are a host of factors that could be shaping thinking, emotions and behaviours at the level of individual and working relationships between professionals and clients. Effective Reflective Practice involves identifying the key factors and working with them to enhance their positive benefits and minimise their negative effects.

## Group-Based Collaborative Reflective Practice

Below we present an outline agenda for a collaborative reflective session, whether in pairs or small groups. If you are familiar with action learning set methodology (Revans, 1982) you may recognise some of the elements.

### Suggested Outline Agenda

- *Check-in:* Invite participants to say briefly how they are feeling entering the session and what they need to leave behind to be in the right frame of mind.
- Establish the *agreed ground rules* for how the session will be organised.
- For groups of three or four decide *who will take the lead in facilitating the conversation* and who will keep proceedings to time.
- *Agree how the time available will be divided* between the participants, ensuring everyone has an equal space to bring their topic to the table.
- *Facilitate the individual time slots*, keeping the focus on the person presenting their topic and providing support and constructive challenge to deepen their reflection and learning.
- *Check-out:* Invite participants to say what they are taking away from the whole conversation, not just their time slot. There will be learning for everyone from others' contributions.

In organising group reflective practice remember another recurring message of this book, namely, to encourage individual and group creativity in the ways topics are presented and explored. The next chapter explores the importance of creativity in reflective practice, and Appendix 3 outlines creative methods that can be adapted for use in pair and group work.

## SUMMARY

This chapter has outlined various ways of encouraging and supporting Effective Reflective Practice in organisational settings. Embracing these ways of embedding intentional practice in professional and organisational contexts can bring multiple benefits.

### The Benefits of Effective Reflective Practice

Effective Reflective Practice is good for professionals because it:

- allows them to enhance their practice whilst also attending to their wellbeing
- encourages them to ensure that their everyday interactions are aligned with their purpose and values.

Effective Reflective Practice is good for clients and stakeholders because it:

- ensures that professionals have their best interests at heart when making enhancements to their service
- provides quality assurance about the professionals who work with them.

*(Continued)*

Effective Reflective Practice is good for organisations because it:

- promotes continuous self-development amongst staff
- underpins a culture of learning, growth and development
- enables important systemic factors affecting their achievements to be identified and explored.

Effective Reflective Practice is good for societies because it:

- supports professionals to be as effective as possible
- nurtures professionals who are engaged and fulfilled in their roles
- establishes a starting point for creativity and innovation in addressing the challenges facing humanity.

## Find Out More

Hawkins, P. & Smith, N. (2013). *Coaching, Mentoring and Organizational Consultancy: Supervision, Skills and Development*. 2nd edn. Maidenhead: Open University Press.

Proctor, B. (2008). *Group Supervision: A Guide to Creative Practice*. 2nd edn. London: Sage.

Revans, R. W. (1982). What is action learning? *Journal of Management Development* 1(3): 64-75.

# 9

# CREATIVITY IN REFLECTIVE PRACTICE

This chapter will cover:

- What is creativity?
- The 'two hemispheres' of the brain
- Creative journaling
- An example of creative reflective practice

In the first eight chapters of this book, we have explored the Effective Reflective Practice framework and how to use it as the foundation for writing about your reflective insights for the purposes of gaining a qualification or professional credentialing. We have also suggested ways Effective Reflective Practice can be incorporated into the work and functioning of organisations. Throughout we have emphasised the benefits to be gained from collaborating with others, alongside learning from your own individual reflections. We have also highlighted the importance of reflecting systemically, while at the same time keeping a prime focus on your relationships with individual clients. As we have indicated, those relationships will be impacted by the context and the thinking, emotions and behaviours of others who have influence over outcomes.

In these chapters we have encouraged you to work systematically through the Effective Reflective Practice framework, especially as you find your feet with the process. In the next chapter, 'The habit of reflective practice', we lay out a number of propositions for integrating reflective practice into your work routine (and life), including becoming freer with the process, imbuing it with your own personal approach. In this chapter, we explore how creativity, including your own existing or emerging creative interests and passions, can provide novel perspectives for your reflective practice. We, the authors, both have a strong visual element to our reflective practice, which we deploy in various ways in our work with clients and organisations. Figure 9.1 captures an example of one of our creative sketches. The chapter is accompanied by Appendix 3, which outlines a range of creative methods you can use to add new dimensions to your reflective activities.

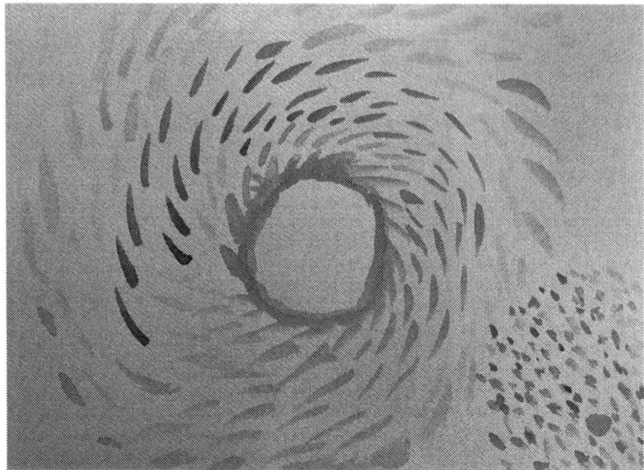

**Figure 9.1** Example of a creative image by one of the authors

## WHAT IS CREATIVITY?

What do you think of when you hear the term 'creativity'? Are you excited about what might be involved or, at the other end of a spectrum, does it generate anxiety about the level of your ability to create? There is a tendency to see creativity as wholly related to the arts and then only of value in the hands of a proficient practitioner – the accomplished artist, musician or actor. In reality, all human activity is creative. Some of you may be reading this thinking, 'I'm not a creative person'. Such inner self-talk should be challenged. *Every* human being is creative. Creativity is found in all fields; it is not the preserve of the artistic endeavours often described as 'creative'. Mathematics and sciences are creative endeavours. They generate technological developments, such as advances in medicine and health interventions. Daniel Levitin (2019), the neuroscientist, describes how in the past all human beings created music, for example, through the songs that communicated important aspects of oral history whereas now music creation has become the preserve of a minority of the population. This has the additional downside that now music is perceived as an activity that requires high degrees of proficiency to be seen as worthwhile.

Some people find it difficult to imagine that creativity might be a way to tackle serious topics, viewing creative activity as too frivolous for such important matters. However, novelist Tom Robbins suggests, 'Humanity has advanced, when it has advanced, not because it has been sober, responsible, and cautious, but because it has been playful, rebellious, and immature' (1980, p. 19). Creativity in reflective practice brings a number of benefits. It:

- makes things visual and therefore easier to see and stand back from
- brings things alive
- unpacks complexity
- introduces playfulness
- enriches people's understanding of their reality
- surfaces the emotions that underpin a particular topic or event
- unearths new perspectives.

Numerous writers attest to the benefits of creativity, which include: sharpening your mind, improving your mood, reducing anxiety and stress, improving wellbeing and mental health, combating depression, enhancing physical health and boosting brain function (e.g. Csikszentmihalyi, 2013; Tan et al., 2021). For example, Stuart Brown asserts that 'The genius of play is that, in playing, we create imaginative new cognitive combinations. And in creating those novel combinations, we find what works' (2010, p. 37).

In their book *The Creative License: Giving Yourself Permission to Be the Artist You Truly Are*, Danny Gregory asserts that 'the ability and need to be creative are hard-wired into all of us … it's a basic urge, an irresistible impulse' (2006, p. 10). They cite examples of people sketching, cooking and making up songs. Sadly, they also point out that despite exhibiting these creative activities many people still believe they are not creative. Ken Robinson (2021) is highly critical of schools and workplaces for their role in shaping this self-perception and stifling creativity. Gregory also debunks a commonly-held misconception that creativity is always about producing something entirely new:

> Creativity doesn't mean just making things up out of thin air. It means seeing and feeling the world so vividly that you can put together connections and patterns that help to explain reality. It means you see the beauty in the world rather than trying to hide from it. (2006, p. 11)

This accords strongly with the purpose of reflective practice, where professionals are endeavouring to see connections and patterns. When you mobilise your own brand of creativity as part of your reflective practice, you will supercharge your learning and gain new insights.

There are many methods that can be used to find new and different ways of thinking, feeling and experiencing. By tapping into your creativity, such methods can be particularly helpful as part of a reflective practice process. This is especially relevant when exploring complicated or difficult topics where the traditional logical, rational and analytical thinking processes may not be producing insights. Given reflective practice is not simply about solving problems, creativity can also be used to generate insights from achievements and successes.

Just as making time for reflective practice requires determination and commitment in the face of many other pressing priorities on your time, carving out the space for creativity within your reflective practice needs effort. In his book *The War of Art*, the author Steven Pressfield (2002) identifies a number of blockages to engaging in creative activities that he calls 'resistances'. These include procrastination, self-doubt, self-criticism and fear of others' critical responses. He goes on to suggest practical ways of overcoming these obstacles to creativity, such as being patient with yourself, establishing even a minimal structure and not taking 'failure' (or success) personally. A lesson we, the authors, have learnt writing books is that when we are suffering from writer's block what works is just writing anything. Getting some words down on the page (or these days the screen) without regard to the quality or relevance of the writing frequently shifts us to a more productive place. We may then end up discarding a significant proportion of what we produce, but in the process we will have broken through the blockage and there will be the kernels of something useful in the remaining debris. So, our advice when you're struggling with any creative activity is to get stuck in, make mistakes and see what emerges that suggests a new direction. As with all skills, setting aside time to practise with a particular creative approach will produce results. You may need to be prepared for fits and starts in the development of your capabilities, rather than expecting straight line, ever-upwards improvement.

When everything really clicks into place creatively, positive psychologists describe the existence of a state of 'flow' (Csikszentmihalyi, 1990). This is when a person is so deeply engaged in an activity that they lose track of time. Being in a state of flow offers personally meaningful rewards and as a result is energising and generates higher performance. In reflective practice not every encounter with a creative approach will produce flow. While achieving flow is desirable, there will still be learning to be gained from creative activities which require greater effort.

## Ways to Achieve Flow

1. Find your core creative interest.
2. Create the right balance of ability and challenge: too much challenge and too little skill will lead to anxiety; too little challenge in relation to a great deal of skill will result in boredom.
3. Remove distractions: make the time and space to focus on a task; What's the best time of day for you? What's the most conducive environment?
4. Make time to practise: boost your skill so you can meet bigger challenges; raise the bar on your expectations of yourself a little each time
5. Seek out new perspectives: get out of your comfort zone to see things differently; what are other people with similar creative interests doing?

In the case of reflective practice, it is worth remembering that the purpose of any associated creative activity is not to exhibit proficiency with the method but to use it to dig deeper into a topic to understand it better and find a way through it. What you create only needs to make sense to yourself, and no-one else. Even if you decide to use your creation in a collaborative conversation with another person, you can explain to them what it means to you and focus together on the insights it provides.

In Chapter 6 we explored learning styles and made the point that it is helpful to have clarity about your preferences. In this way you will be able to deploy your strengths effectively in your reflective practice. We have underlined the importance of tapping into your capabilities to further your professional development. We have also emphasised the importance of moving out of your comfort zones and adopting learning styles that are not how you would usually approach things. Though potentially discomforting at first, this will offer very different and valuable perspectives. Chapter 6 also outlined the VARK learning styles, which lend themselves well to thinking about how you might prefer to engage with creative approaches to reflective practice. If you have a visual preference, it is likely that you will be drawn to visually creative methods like doodling, sketching or painting. Alternatively, an auditory learning style preference will mean you are likely to gain benefits from engaging with sound-based approaches, perhaps related to music, speaking out loud and the sounds of nature (such as birdsong). Professionals with an inclination towards the reading and writing preference will gain inspiration from writing imaginary letters, creating haikus and limericks and reading poetry and literature. Finally, kinaesthetic learners will enjoy tactile activities such as mapping, modelling and drawing on activities that involve moving objects around. Of course, as we have stressed, human beings rarely utilise just one single learning style and, once again, we encourage you to experiment both with those styles that are comfortable and those to which you would perhaps normally give a wide berth. Staying in your comfort zone risks complacency while moving too far away from it can lead to stress. However, some discomfort is what might provide you with new insights and a different perspective through which to create and view your reflections. There is no need for you to be proficient in the methods you decide to use. For instance, if you are using an art-based approach, there is no expectation that you should create an artistic masterpiece. Using this method is not a test of your artistic ability but rather an opportunity for you to create your own 'visual language' (Sheather, 2019) which you alone need to understand and see. Just give it a go and see what emerges!

## THE 'TWO HEMISPHERES' OF THE BRAIN

It has long been held that the two hemispheres of the brain have different functions. 'Left brain' activity involves logical and rational thought while the 'right brain' offers potential for creativity. Neuroscience is indicating that this distinction is more complex and the relationship between the vital roles of each hemisphere is important, for example, in much human activity, including creative endeavour. However, it is clear that left brain activity, relying on cognition, is the default position adopted by most human beings especially when they are faced with a challenge. This tendency is further encouraged by the structures and processes operating in the systems in which people live and work. In the main, for instance, the education system prioritises and rewards logical, rational thinking over more creative ways of approaching the world. This dominance of left brain thinking continues into the work environment where taking creative approaches is seen as, at best, irrelevant and time-wasting and, at worst, as childish and risky. Clearly, logical and rational approaches are essential aspects of reflective practice. Indeed, our Effective Reflective Practice framework is based on a logical and rational cycle. *And*, we argue, tapping into the potential of the right brain to generate fresh and novel ideas is equally of value. Given the existential challenges facing humanity (such as the climate emergency, poverty and inequality), creativity and innovation, we believe, are a vital part of the solutions. As Albert Einstein famously suggested: it is futile trying to solve problems using the very thinking that created them.

When professionals want to engage in creative approaches to reflective practice, they intentionally take steps to minimise, or eliminate the dominance of the left brain and move away from 'thinking' as the only way to gain insights. Mindfulness and meditative exercises can be very helpful in slowing down thought and allowing creativity to flourish. Anna Sheather, who is also an artist and coach, asserts that:

> ... art can be very effective in quieting the left hemisphere and allowing the right hemisphere to take over the task ... the image-making process externalises and makes visible the right hemisphere's experiences and perceptions. The art my clients create give[s] their right hemisphere a voice through, not only the image, but also the language of the image making process. This enables them to access the non-verbal, unconscious parts of their internal world, externalising the complex, paradoxical and the hidden. They are able to hold the whole of it just as it is, in all its complexity.
> (2019, p. 36)

Betty Edwards (2008), along with many other artists, underlines the benefits of drawing as a way of slowing down left brain thinking and allowing the right hemisphere to become dominant. We, the authors, prefer to use the term 'sketching', as people's perception of drawing is often one which involves high levels of technical, representational skill. Doodling and random mark-making involve no 'artistic' skill and serve the purpose of quieting the verbal, analytical left brain very effectively enabling the left-to-right brain shift. Tom Granger (2019) focuses on using simple sketching techniques allied with a focus on breathing as a means of creating a meditative state which enables right brain activity to come to the fore.

1. Take a piece of A4 paper and a pencil, crayon or other mark-making implement.
2. Focus on your breath; breathe in slowly and then out slowly, making the out-breath slightly longer than the in-breath.
3. Place your pencil in one corner of the sheet of paper.
4. As you breathe in allow your pencil to make a line across the page for the length of your in-breath.
5. Keep your pencil on the paper and as you breathe out make a line down the page for the length of your out-breath.
6. Repeat this 'drawing breath' (Granger, 2019) process for five minutes.
7. As you sketch your lines, what do you notice about your breath and what happens in your mind?
8. To use this process as part of your creative reflective practice, between Steps 1 and 2 decide on a topic you would like to focus on; what emerges about this topic by the end of the 'drawing breath' process?

Simple cartoons can be a rich source of reflection and insight. Using stick figures, basic shapes and speech and thought bubbles, a scenario can be depicted and explored. Cartooning is a very effective way of exaggerating the absurdities of life, enabling them to be examined in more detail and resolutions identified. In the example in Figure 9.2, a professional wanted to help a client to explore the gap between the espoused values of a workplace and people's daily lived experience. Creating the cartoon crystallised the key issues in play and enabled the client to decide constructive ways for improving the situation. These involved, for example, using their 'expert power' (i.e. the authority they have as a result of their specialist expertise) and constructive strategies for encouraging more openness and authenticity in working relationships.

**Figure 9.2** Cartoon created to reflect on inauthentic leadership

Of course, you can always create cartoons that are more polished, as in Figure 9.3.

**Figure 9.3** Revised inauthentic leadership cartoon

## CREATIVE JOURNALING

As we have suggested earlier in this book, journaling is a powerful way of generating and capturing your reflections. Journals can comprise notes about your thoughts, feelings and ideas. This form of written journaling is creative in itself in that you can, for example, use various styles of writing or different coloured pens to distinguish different topics and themes. You can also include doodles and other visual embellishments to make particular words and phrases stand out, such as using circling, underlining and highlighter pens. In addition, you can expand the level of creativity by using a variety of mark-making instruments, paint, stickers, collage and incorporating found objects into the pages.

Creative journaling is a space to have a conversation with yourself about any aspect of your work or life that you wish to explore, including your inner musings. As a safe and private place to capture your thoughts and emotions, it becomes a record of your reflections and your growth over time. Creative journaling has a number of demonstrable benefits, including:

- a visual means of noticing patterns in your thinking, emotions and behaviour
- problem identification, prioritisation and resolution
- a memory aid capturing events, feelings and details that become pertinent to later reflections
- a place to process difficulties or sensitivities associated with challenges, anxieties or stress
- wellbeing enhancement through the recording of the things you are thankful for (gratitude journaling) and boosting your confidence
- opportunities for positive self-talk and addressing negative self-perceptions
- the identification, setting and monitoring of personal and professional goals
- improved self-management and becoming better organised.

The book you choose for your journal needs some thought. Ideally it should have thick paper that will not lead to ink or paint bleeding through to the next page and can take the weight of the cut-outs and found items you will want to glue into it. There are, of course, digital options and it is perfectly possible to create a journal on your laptop or tablet using cut and paste images. However, we believe the physical act of creating a journal with your own hands has a quality to it which can be lost in the digital space, just as writing with a pen and paper can feel more personal than working on a laptop. To make the journal truly your own you can decorate the cover in whatever way you like. What 'look' will motivate you to pick up and add to your journal on a frequent and regular basis?

Facing the blank page can be daunting. This can be overcome by painting the page with a base colour to which you can then add text, sketches and pictures. The key thing is not to be too precious about your journal. Acknowledge any 'mistakes' and embrace them, incorporating these apparent aberrations into a revised creation that suits your reflective purposes. If you need them, you can find a wide range of journaling templates on the internet. These provide prompts to stimulate your initial reflections and get you started.

We encourage you to be as free as possible with how you create in your journal. When you are writing notes forget about being precise and correct with your spelling, punctuation and grammar. It can help to write quickly and without back-tracking for revisions. If you get stuck for words, turn to doodling, sketching or collaging. When you are creating images, avoid judging your artistic skill. Simply recreate as best you can what comes to mind. Mindfulness and visualisation exercises can help to quell your thoughts and allow images to emerge. Anything goes. There is no wrong way to journal creatively, whatever works for you is the right way, and that can change at any point as you see fit. This is your own safe and private space to indulge your meanderings and see where they lead. Experiment with a diverse array of media … and be kind to yourself by avoiding judgement about what you create. Turn your inner critic into a critical friend (see Figure 9.4) by noticing, without doubting yourself, what their voice might be telling you that you need to acknowledge.

**Figure 9.4** Image created by David Love to reflect on his Dracula-like inner critic

Creative journaling can be a form of storytelling (see Figure 9.5). What are the stories you want to explore in your journal either through words or imagery, or both? Journaling your story in the third person can sometimes be helpful in creating a separation between yourself and the events that enables reflection about the salient points to come more easily.

To make creative journaling a habit it is worth giving some thought to how you will incorporate spending time with your journal into your schedule. How often will you journal? At what point in the day do you find reflective practice more conducive to your mood? What regular time works best for your motivation to keep the creative journaling going?

**Figure 9.5** Collage created by David focusing on moving forward with his work

Finally, what are your creative interests and passions? What do you spend time doing in your private life that is creative, bearing in mind the very broad definition of creativity we are putting forward in this chapter? For example, do you paint? Are you really into music? Do you write poetry? Are you a great cook or gardener? Perhaps you excel at crosswords or number puzzles? How might you utilise these capabilities in your reflective practice?

## An Example of Creative Reflective Practice

I am a leadership coach and coach supervisor who uses art-based methods in my work with clients and in my own regular professional reflective practice. I am currently undertaking the ART in Coaching ADCT accredited Diploma in Art-based Coaching and an integral part of the programme is a commitment to personal and professional development through creative reflective practice. The programme has been designed and led by Anna Sheather, and I am using her structured Creative Reflective Process (Sheather, 2023), which is based on her Five Stages of Art in Coaching framework (Sheather, 2019).

In the example of reflective practice presented here I explored a key aspect of coaching and supervision and considered the particular impacts of engaging with clients using an art-based approach.

I wanted to focus my creative reflective practice on how to offer constructive challenge to clients in an art-based session where they may feel especially vulnerable because (a) they are unused to using art in a professional context, (b) they have reservations about their ability to create an image and/or (c) they have revealed, through the creation of an image, emotions that would otherwise have remained hidden. Finding ways to offer constructive challenge in such a potentially charged context makes the need for sensitivity and empathy on the part of the coach even more vital.

I decided to start my creative reflective activity by using Jeanette Cowley's *Voicing Possibilities* images. It is important to note that I had no preconceived ideas about where this activity was going to lead. Rather, I was prepared to see what emerged as the process unfolded in whatever directions the imagery might take me.

I chose 12 images from the *Voicing Possibilities* pack. The number was random, though I felt comfortable with an even rather than an odd number. I was drawn to images with strong colours - rich reds, greens, pinks, etc. I am a very visual person and often find myself looking for patterns and connections in what I see in the world around me. As a result, I arranged the cards to make connections based on linking the same colours, which resulted in the configuration shown in Figure 9.6.

*(Continued)*

**Figure 9.6** Arranging cards

Looking at this layout I had a strong desire to photograph it and accentuate the colour connections by painting over them with watercolours on a printout. This led to a second image (Figure 9.7).

**Figure 9.7** Painting over cards

Looking carefully, it is possible to see the *Voicing Possibilities* cards under the paint.

(For the purposes of this book we have recreated Figure 9.7 as a black and white image – see Figure 9.8. A full colour version can be found as part of the online materials accompanying this book: https://study.sagepub.com/nieuwerburghlove1e).

**Figure 9.8** Black & white version of Figure 9.7

Up to this point I continued to have no preconceived ideas about where all this might be heading. It is essential in the creative reflective process not to get drawn into reaching conclusions before a detailed exploration of the images has been undertaken. Connecting to an image involves not allowing the rational, logical, thinking brain to rush ahead to answers. Instead, allowing the emotional, creative side of the brain to make connections to the image provides a rich underpinning and stimulus for later insights and learning.

Over several days in which I kept returning to the images for short periods I began to see significance in the different colours (Table 9.1).

## Reflecting on What Emerged

I need to be even more courageous, open and clear about the importance of challenge and its benefits for clients. This would open up opportunities for a clearer dialogue with clients about the detail of what challenge in a coaching conversation might look like for them.

*(Continued)*

The blue (thick horizontal lines in Figure 9.8) is a vital feature of the image. My ability to create calm, safe coaching environments is an anchor in my relationships creating strong bonds of trust and enabling me to offer challenge constructively as well as manage any responses from clients, whatever form those may take. It will be important to have more faith and confidence in this personal strength.

There are two creative people in the room. Drawing on our respective creative abilities, however they manifest themselves, is another strong foundation on which to base a relationship that encourages and fosters constructive challenge.

Finally, part of the image (reproduced in Figure 9.9) looks like a face - or a mask. This raised a question for me about whether my ability to create strong trusting connections with clients is a performance rather than my authentic response to another human being. Based on feedback from clients, colleagues, family and friends (and my own values and beliefs) I am confident that the blue (thick horizontal lines in Figure 9.8) reflects a genuine feature of my humanity.

**Table 9.1** Significance of colours

| Colour | My interpretation of the significance |
|---|---|
| Black | The darkness and perils associated with me getting a challenge wrong; the potentially damaging elements that might undermine the all-important relationship I have with a client |
| Red (vertical stripes in Figure 9.8) | The ways a client might respond emotionally to a challenge that I notice – through their words, facial expressions, demeanour and body language |
| Pink (thin horizontal lines in Figure 9.8) | The ways a client might respond emotionally to a challenge that it is impossible for me to see – these may be very powerful, and because they are unseen, less amenable to being managed |
| Green (spots in Figure 9.8) | The creativity of both myself and the client – as a resource for managing challenge |
| Brown (white in Figure 9.8) | The fertile ground (soil) for a productive relationship |
| Silver/grey (diagonal stripes in Figure 9.8) | The silver lining in a challenge (i.e. the actual and potential benefits the client gains – plus my purposeful intention to 'do good') |
| Yellow (cross hatch in Figure 9.8) | The occasions when I might hold back a challenge ('cowardice') in order to avoid potential difficulties |
| Blue (thick horizontal lines in Figure 9.8) | The calm, steady holding I bring to a client relationship – a strong element of my approach, which is frequently reflected back to me in feedback from clients; in the image this feels like a foundation underpinning the other elements |

**Figure 9.9** Face or mask?

This was an extremely valuable piece of creative reflective practice, which led to a number of insightful learnings, including:

- Increased acknowledgement that challenge in the coaching context can clearly take many forms. In art-based coaching, it is vital to take care not to offer any interpretation of the client's image. That image belongs to them (and is an extension of them) and the coach's interpretations, or reinterpretations will disrupt their own understanding of their creation. An assumption made by the coach can generate an unnecessary and potentially undermining challenge for the client.
- Recognition that I have significant strengths (e.g. in creating a calm and safe environment) which provide a foundation for even more courageous challenge.
- Strengthening of the importance of a contract with clients that creates greater clarity about how the client understands challenge and their expectations about what that feels like in reality.

## SUMMARY

In this chapter we have highlighted the benefits that can be gained from taking creative approaches to your reflective practice. We have emphasised that all human beings (and human activity) are creative. We have shown how you can draw on a wide array of creative possibilities and have encouraged you to use your own creative interests and passions in your reflective activities and journaling. Appendix 3 comprises a number of creative methods you can use, on your own or in collaboration with others. We encourage you to try these out, even those that generate an initial negative response in you. The purpose of using creativity in reflective practice is to find different and new ways of seeing and thus gain insights that would otherwise remain hidden. Experiment and adapt. What creative approaches can you invent that work for you?

## Find Out More

Gregory, D. (2006). *The Creative License: Giving Yourself Permission to Be the Artist You Truly Are*. New York: Hachette.

Robinson, K. (2001). *Out of Our Minds: Learning to Be Creative*. Oxford: Capstone Publishing.

Sheather, A. (2019). *Coaching Beyond Words: Using Art to Deepen and Enrich Our Conversations*. Abingdon: Routledge.

Sheather, A. (2023). Creative Reflective Practice: A Guide to Creative Reflective Art Journaling. Association for Coaching Diploma in Art-based Coaching course materials.

Wheeler, S. & Leyman, T. (2024). *Playfulness in Coaching: Exploring Our Untapped Potential through Playfulness, Creativity and Imagination*. Abingdon: Routledge.

For more information about the *Voicing Possibilities* Cards visit Jeanette Cowley's website: goforgrowth.com

# 10

# THE HABIT OF REFLECTIVE PRACTICE

This chapter will cover:

- Ten propositions for making reflective practice a habit:
  - Start with intention
  - Develop theories and test them
  - Access as much information as possible
  - Reflect in the moment
  - Do the right thing
  - Connect to meaning and purpose
  - Pay attention to your wellbeing
  - Seek out support
  - Hold the process lightly
  - Integrate reflection into your everyday practice
- Making the propositions come to life
- Living intentionally

Our intention in writing this book has been to set out a clearly structured, easy-to-follow framework for reflective practice. In the interests of clarity, the process is presented as linear; each phase presented as distinct and independent of the others; and it appears that professionals should not skip any part of it. At the same time, we are strong advocates of integrating Effective Reflective Practice into our everyday lives.

As we have discovered in the process of writing this book and through our own professional practice, processes of reflective practice can become central to the ways in which people live their lives. This chapter is intended to facilitate the process of integration. As you cycle through the Effective Reflective Practice framework numerous times, much of it will become familiar. In essence, it is a process of being clear about your intentions; thinking about what could be different; planning for a better future; trying things out; and then using that learning to inform the next cycle.

Once you are comfortable using the Effective Reflective Practice framework, it becomes possible to adopt this process as a way of interacting and being in the world. This chapter brings together the insights of experienced professionals who have integrated reflective practice seamlessly into their everyday lives. We interviewed a group of professionals including artists, a leader, academics, a social worker, a coach, a health professional and a business consultant. We interviewed these practitioners to support us with the development and articulation of the Effective Reflective Practice framework. In this chapter, we share some of their insights with you. To be as helpful and as explicit as possible, we have positioned their insights under ten propositions that have emerged through writing this book and from real practice (see Table 10.1).

**Table 10.1** Ten propositions for making reflective practice a habit

| | |
|---|---|
| 1 | Start with intention |
| 2 | Develop theories and test them |
| 3 | Access as much information as possible |
| 4 | Reflect in the moment |
| 5 | Do the right thing |
| 6 | Connect to meaning and purpose |
| 7 | Pay attention to your wellbeing |
| 8 | Seek out support |
| 9 | Hold the process lightly |
| 10 | Integrate reflection into your everyday practice |

## PROPOSITION 1: START WITH INTENTION

The Effective Reflective Practice framework emphasises the importance of starting with an intention. Being clear about the focus of your reflective practice will provide you with a clear sense of purpose, shaping the outcome you wish to achieve and mapping your travel through the rest of the framework.

Our interviewees illustrated how having clarity about your intention at the start supports the entire reflective process. While one of the experienced practitioners says they do not follow a particular method for their reflections, they highlight that their practice is always intentional:

> I'm familiar with some of the models of reflective practice, but I've never been a great one for painting by numbers. I think I'm always reflecting, you know, it's just the way I'm structured. I'm always kind of thinking things through, thinking about things that have happened and seeing whether, you know, there might have been a different way of doing it. I do [reflect] intentionally, but I don't do it in a structured way.

In contrast, another respondent relies on a clear framework for their reflective practice. The starting point for their approach involves going back to 'first principles':

> Learning for me is very often revisiting things I already know and allowing them to embed and enrich further. As a professional, I have a framework in mind of where I can go in that moment and stop and say, right, what am I doing? It is helpful to go back to first principles.

A third respondent's reflective practice intentions are founded on their view of professionalism, which focuses on the question: 'Is the right person doing the right thing at the right time?':

> I end up having something that's an intention, like letting go of something that I'm stuck on at the moment or it might be a feeling or it might be a difficult moment with a person, or it might be something that's coming up that I want to visualize how I want this interaction to go. Or it might be a piece of art or something that is either already there, or I'm wanting to envision a feeling of it, and then I often will use [my reflective time] just by noticing what keeps coming up around that feeling.

Another respondent emphasises the centrality of a connection between an intention in reflective practice and a practitioner's wider professional purpose:

> To me there's something intentional about it [reflective practice]. So I mean we can all think about things that we did. It is only reflective practice when we ask 'what is our *intent*?'

## PROPOSITION 2: DEVELOP THEORIES AND TEST THEM

A key element of the Effective Reflective Practice framework is the development and testing of theories. We have written about the importance of having an hypothesis (or hypotheses) about the outcome you are seeking from your reflection and of the need to devise and implement experiments to test this thinking in reality.

One respondent described the intricacies of checking on their hypotheses:

> One is capturing information all the time, both visually, cerebrally through talking and thinking and taking on board what one is doing … and getting that down with good notekeeping and then testing the theory. So the structure is there and you're continually reflecting.

Testing out theories plays an important part of their reflective practice:

> I'm always reflecting on what I do in practice in relation to each patient that I see. First of all, I'm testing my theories. Am I being ethical? Am I being safe? If I'm seeing somebody over a period of time, I should be reflecting why I'm seeing them, what the outcomes are and keeping good notes.

One of the practitioners explained how they are theorising all the time:

> Something will come into my mind: It was really interesting that he said such and such. That makes me think about something. Sometimes, I'll go and get their folders out and put a note in for next time, because I've thought about something to do with somebody. So I do have a framework that's embedded around the concept of affirming what's working well, asking questions about what can I do more of or differently, and [then reflect on] the impact on particular people.

As part of their testing process, another respondent revisits their reflections:

> I've reflected once and I'm going back and reflecting again. I might reflect the first time and miss some detail, and when I do it the second time, I might bring to memory something that I don't remember. I would go back and say, is that a whole picture? Did I capture everything? It's a way of just making sure that I haven't missed anything.

Another practitioner concluded that: 'reflective practice is … a meta kind of approach where we think about action, reflect on it, and then use that … to learn for the next time'.

## PROPOSITION 3: ACCESS AS MUCH INFORMATION AS POSSIBLE

Your reflective practice will be at its most effective if you tap into as many sources of information as possible. One source of information will be the facts about a situation. These may or may not be verifiable and may, of course, be your perceptions, which are just as important for your reflections. Your thoughts about a situation are clearly an important source of information and, as we have stressed throughout this book, how you feel will also provide a rich source of learning. 'Emotions are data' as one of the experienced practitioners says in their interview. They pay acute attention to their feelings as an integral part of their approach:

> What emotions do I attach to that event or the experience? I generally see emotions as data telling me something. What is it telling me? I also look underneath for what was evoking the emotion.

A second respondent reports that reflective practice has allowed them to be more 'emotionally aware of how I come across to people'.

This is a point made strongly by another person we interviewed: 'In immediately reaching for a tick box sheet are [people] forgetting about that emotional feeling which is a response to their particular work?'

Finding imaginative ways to reflect can provide new and insightful perspectives. One of the respondents describes how they achieve this:

> I walk backwards and forwards all the time. So, you know, I think I [am] probably standing away from the work more than I'm up against it. But I also have a mirror in the corner of the studio. I can look at it and I can look at the work in that. It reverses the image and I can see more clearly, particularly problems with the design. I can see those much more clearly by looking into the mirror. So having done that, I can then make a much better decision on what I must do next. And so I move on from there.

Another practitioner reported how they draw on Zen Buddhism and other spiritual disciplines:

> I talk to my pastor. I go to those more contemplative disciplines for reflection. You know, when he speaks, for example, about specific Bible verses you can [gain insights from] them. And then we reflect on it together. You don't need to be specifically religious to say, this is a helpful verse from the Bible that helps me reflect on my ethics, but also my way of being.

Another respondent's reflective practice also involves a creative approach: 'I like playing the movies of my professional performance to myself, with the lens of appreciative inquiry and the philosophy of kaizen, which is a Japanese word for continuous improvement.'

The notion of an 'internal dialogue' is raised by one of our respondents:

> I think the most important aspect of it for me is that we're conscious and aware of what we're doing, and conscious and aware of what we want to do in future, and especially what's going on inside of us when we're doing things right. So, it's not just the content of what's happened, but also especially from the Buddhist perspective, what effect does it have on me and why does it have that effect on me?

Accessing diverse sources of information will enable you to gain a sense of what is really important. One of our interviewees spoke about how we develop this notion through reflective practice:

> The longer I have been doing work in this area and doing it myself, the less I feel like I know, and the more I feel like I come to this from a place of extraordinary practice and intellectual humility. Being an ongoing learner myself creating a space in between action and reaction shapes how we pay attention and what we pay attention to, and lets us have tools for our integration of self and knowledge and response. I'm a person who experiences the world in a very physical and relational kind of way. I notice information first in my body, in my throat and my voice.

Another described looking for differences that might have impacted a particular situation:

> What might those differences be? Are they related to age or generational differences? Am I working with someone from a sector I'm not familiar with? Am I unfamiliar with the kind of work they do? Are they presenting an issue that I don't have much experience of engaging with? I like to get to as much detail as possible in my reflection in order to establish whether there is a need for change, there is a need for improvement, or to just celebrate what I've done as being good enough.

The value of noticing how other people react to you was also highlighted:

> I can monitor what's going on in the audience and I can adapt. I'll change tack, perhaps in the middle of something, if I feel the energy level going down or I've gone off track or I'm getting a negative vibe. What I'm doing is I'm taking feedback from people, from the body language, the nonverbal cues. I'm trying to get a sense of how things are landing. I often get to a conference, maybe two speakers before [my slot] and sit indoors and get a sense of the audience.

A very effective way of widening your sources of information is to seek feedback and share ideas with colleagues. One respondent is 'always conscious about growth and how I can get better. I like to share my findings, successes, queries with my colleagues, which I find very valuable.'

## PROPOSITION 4: REFLECT IN THE MOMENT (NOT JUST ON THE MOMENT)

The Effective Reflective Practice framework was designed as a process for reflecting on professional practice, before and after interactions. However, the experienced reflective practitioners we interviewed talked about reflecting *in the moment*. According to them, once reflective practice becomes a habit, it is possible to deploy reflection *during* our interactions, too.

Here is one of the respondents talking about this kind of in-the-moment reflection:

> I find myself often reflecting and observing myself in action whilst in the moment when I'm delivering, whether I'm delivering a lecture, I'm in a workshop. I kind of scan myself for how I'm feeling about what I'm doing and also rely on emotions in terms of seeing it as data for me. What is it telling me, either from the people that I'm engaging with, the environment or the space that I'm in, and also myself? How am I feeling about what's going on for me?
>
> I'm someone who keeps a lot of mental notes. When I am in action or doing something. … I've gotten better at being hyper self-aware. When I'm in a space where all eyes are on me, I'm the one actually delivering something, I'm always kind of scanning to … check the reaction from the people I'm engaging with. This could be, you know, facial expressions, the body language – it doesn't have to be words. And I'm just kind of cataloguing that away … and if we do have a break in the session, then I've already made that mental note of who I'm going to go and speak with and why I want to speak to them. It could be maybe when I mention something they made a face or they kind of … shifted in a certain way. I'll find a gentle way to go in and … explore the reaction that I noticed. And at the end of the session, I make it a point of duty not to leave the venue until I've sat down to just do a quick summary of key things that I want to delve deeper into. So it's usually mostly relying on my own mental notes. I believe that skill has sharpened and been better based on experience and the number of times I've done it. I've done it over and over again.

Similar thoughts were shared by another experienced practitioner:

> I was always able to speak, but I think I got a lot better at it when I started to be able to do in-action monitoring of what was going on in the presentation. So I'm able to divide my attention between what I'm presenting, what you say and what's going on in the audience.

One of the respondents also shared some of the 'in-the-moment' questions that they engage with: 'What does it say about me? Where does it come from? How do I want to use this moment? How do I want to transform the emotions that came up there?'

In all three cases, the skill of 'in-the-moment' or 'in-action' reflection is seen as a professional advantage that leads to better outcomes. The challenge, of course, is that it is taking place in the midst of something else. In our view, this is why it is important that the essential skills of reflective practice are developed first, in relatively quiet and focused environments. The aim is for reflective practice to become integral to how we operate as human beings.

## PROPOSITION 5: DO THE RIGHT THING

The core elements of ethical professional practice are:

- Do no harm
- Pay attention to your duty of care, acting in ways that promote wellbeing
- Know your limits, working within your areas of competence
- Respect the interests of your client
- Act within the law.

These underpinning principles sit behind ethical standards expected by your professional body and the legal system in your country.

One respondent highlights the importance of noticing the harmful impacts of stereotyping in their reflective practice:

> We know from research that when an academic from a minority background is teaching students there could be an environment of challenge from those students, almost kind of seeing [the academic] as having less authority or knowledge of their subject area, even when there is no evidence to confirm that. So therefore, the students might engage differently. [For example there can be different responses] to a black female academic teaching them versus a white male who they see as a figure of leadership and authority.

Another is determined to be an ethical practitioner:

> I have interesting moments in my professional role. When it's something about ethics, it's something where I feel I noticed something in myself. I noticed a reaction in myself when I had a specific moment. What does it say about me? Where does it come from? How do I want to use this moment? How do I want to transform the emotions that came up there? Those are really, really deep discussions sometimes.

## PROPOSITION 6: CONNECT TO MEANING AND PURPOSE

The people that we interviewed often connected to their meaning and purpose through reflective practice. The Effective Reflective Practice framework aims to harness the benefits of doing so by starting with a positive intention. At its core, reflective practice is an opportunity to learn about ourselves and enhance our interactions with the world around us.

During one interview it emerged that reflective practice allows practitioners to live 'fully':

> I love my reflective practice. It makes me feel more and more alive. You know, to meditate, to talk about my meditation practice, to live according to the brahmavihara – the four noble truths. And my reflective practice helps me be more confident in doing that in my life. Life is where it's happening, right? Life and reflective practice are not separate. Life is your reflective practice, and at the same time, your reflective practice is making you feel more fully alive.

One respondent reported that they never really thought of themselves as a 'reflective practitioner':

> I just thought of myself as wanting to get unstuck from things. The cognition wasn't getting me there, and I'm actually surprised to hear myself say this and then realize, 'wow, I've like been doing that for 20 years in ways that actually have made my life much more meaningful'.

Another puts it simply when they say 'reflective practice allows one to just feel fulfilled – that one is doing things to the best of one's ability'.

## PROPOSITION 7: PAY ATTENTION TO YOUR WELLBEING

When we set out to write this book, we were committed to developing a framework for reflective practice that took into account the wellbeing of the professional and their stakeholders. Wellbeing is an integral element of Effective Reflective Practice based on the premise that people can be of greater service to others when they are at their best.

Reflective practice can support wellbeing in a number of ways. First, it can allow practitioners to acknowledge what they are doing well. For example, one respondent noted that as a result of reflective practice, 'I can feel confident. I feel pleased that I can see those things that tell me that I'm working well.' Second, reflective practice can be a way of alleviating stress, as another experienced practitioner explains: 'I've seen the pattern before, so I don't get knocked off my stride. ... Because while I'm watching what's happening, I'm reflecting on the fact I've actually seen this before, and I know how this goes. I know how this plays out. And I find that really helpful. So I don't suffer much from stress anymore.'

Third, reflective practice can be an important opportunity to check in on our wellbeing. Here are some reflections on how conversations with peers can be helpful:

> And I think as humans, it's really important to acknowledge that because we're all busy and often we don't have the space in order to think ... 'okay, I'm really tired today'. And actually, is that impacting on the decisions that I'm making in a work environment? And I think often it is. So being able to explore that with people is really important.

This respondent concludes by asking a powerful question: 'If we don't look after ourselves, then how can we look after other people?'

## PROPOSITION 8: SEEK OUT SUPPORT

Frequently, our interviewees mentioned the importance of a social support network as they engaged with reflective practice. While everyone valued individual reflection and exploration of ideas, there was considerable support for involving others in the process. This is an opportunity for you to decide what kind of support network you will need as you become a more experienced reflective practitioner.

In some cases, a peer arrangement seems to be very effective, as this quote elucidates:

> That conversation that we have with each other about each other's work is an important part of the reflective process, our own reflective process in the studio. Again, that's really intriguing because one of our thoughts is that much more can emerge if you do this in collaboration with somebody. Yeah. And it's not a process where you go away in a darkened room and kind of think very hard. It can happen quickly and much more effectively if you're in conversation with somebody else.

One of the experienced practitioners notes how they use a tradition from Zen Buddhism as part of their reflective practice. Talking about a *sangha* (a community of practitioners), they explain that:

> ... usually it takes a minimum of five people to do that. The practice of *dharma* sharing is that you sit in a circle and you bow towards the circle if you want to share anything. And usually you share something on your spiritual journey, on your spiritual practice, like how did it go with the practice? What did you struggle with? What did you notice? And the point of dharma sharing is just to share, and everyone else is listening with

> compassion. It's not about advice giving. It's not about direct response to the other person.

One of the respondents highlights how important it is to have social support:

> If you reflect individually rather than with somebody else, you can start to just look at the negatives or the flaws rather than drawing out the positives, and it becomes an internal conversation rather than an external conversation. … I think it's more helpful to have somebody who's facilitating that conversation in order for you to be able to get that kind of real, deep, meaningful reflection that you need.

## PROPOSITION 9: HOLD THE PROCESS LIGHTLY

This book has emphasised the importance of having a clear framework for your reflective practice. We believe we have created a structure that will guide you through your reflections without constraining how you personally use the framework. Depending on your circumstances and experience of reflective practice you can decide to stay close to the process of the framework. Alternatively, as the illustrations from the experienced reflective practitioners we interviewed highlight, you can hold the framework loosely.

All of our respondents in their different ways pointed to forms of reflection that do not just involve sitting and thinking. One described how being outdoors is a stimulus for their reflections:

> I'm not a 'sit on a cushion and do reflection' kind of person. I love walks, I love walking and unpacking or disentangling something that's complex. I absolutely love walking labyrinths. I love the idea that we don't really know. I never know how close I am to the centre or how close I am to the way out either. Labyrinths are a physical way of doing reflection. And I'm still learning a lot about making decisions about building reflective space into my work–life balance from a place that creates more freedom.

Other respondents commented on how they are constantly tapping into their creativity:

> I suppose it's something about being a creative person that one can't help creating. You can't stop creating.

The creation and use of visual imagery are vital ways we, the authors, engage in reflective practice.

## PROPOSITION 10: INTEGRATE REFLECTION INTO YOUR EVERYDAY PRACTICE

One of the most important ways of integrating effective reflective practice into how we typically think is to make it part of your regular routine. In the initial stages, it is necessary to learn and follow the Effective Reflective Practice framework closely. This is similar to learning any new process. However, with time and experience, professionals can adapt, abbreviate or alter elements of the framework to better integrate it into their everyday practice.

Most of the experienced professionals we spoke to suggested that reflective practice had become a habit for them. One acknowledged that 'I do it kind of all the time. It's very random and it's stimulated by different things.' For them, 'that kind of process is happening all the time'. Another respondent expressed a similar view. They are 'always conscious about growth and how I can get better' and acknowledge that 'reflection is very much ongoing all the time'. Many of our respondents suggested that reflective practice had become second nature: 'And so whatever one is doing, whether it's housework or gardening or hanging out washing, there's always that thing in the back of your mind.'

Some professions have reflective practice integrated into their initial training making it easier for people to continue the process once they have qualified. One of the practitioners we interviewed talked about how for them reflective practice, particularly through professional supervision, has become a straightforward routine:

> It's embedded through our three-year degree or apprenticeship. I think because I've been within a reflective profession for so long it's almost innate with what I do. I'm really passionate about supervision and about the positives that it can bring to the workforce. I think I am a[n] innately reflective person and I love reflection.

Another practitioner explained that reflection is a continuous process:

> I just find that my reflection is something that is really going on all the time in the sense that it's triggered by all sorts of different things.

One practitioner highlighted that a vital part of their reflective habit involves collaborative reflection with others:

> I love to get away with a colleague and be out of town or something. I'll call and say: Would you like to spend a day walking and just talk about our ideas?

## MAKING THE PROPOSITIONS COME TO LIFE

In this chapter we have indicated, through illustrations of reflective practitioners in action, that over time and with experience the framework can become second nature and blend into the background. It will always be there to be foregrounded again when needed. As one of our respondents states, when they get stuck, they go back to the foundational principles of their professional development. In the same way, the Effective Reflective Practice framework will be there for you to use when a particular challenge requires you to work through something in a carefully structured way.

We have created a structured framework to scaffold your reflective practice and we are encouraging you to find your own creative ways of engaging in reflective practice to make the approach your own. The propositions in this chapter are a guide to the key elements required for establishing and maintaining a reflective habit. As you have seen from our interviews, making these propositions come to life can be achieved in myriad ways. What particular passions do you have that you could put to good use as part of integrating the framework into your work and life?

### Appreciation for those Who Agreed to be Interviewed

We, the authors, are incredibly grateful to the experienced professionals who generously gave their time to talk to us about the nuances of their approaches to reflective practice. The following professionals have shaped our thinking about the Effective Reflective Practice framework and provided valuable insights for this chapter:

- Nick Andrew and Tanya Hinton, Artists
- Daraius Cooper, Cranial Osteopath
- Kate Cuthbertson, Social Worker, Practice Educator and Supervisor
- Prof. Ashley Duggan, Social Scientist and Communication Expert
- Di Henning, Senior Consultant and Coach Supervisor
- Dr Nelly Nyugen, Executive Coach and Leadership Expert
- Prof. Ciaran O'Boyle, Director of the Centre for Positive Health Sciences
- Dr Jummy Okoya, Academic and Interim Dean of Office for Institutional Equity

## LIVING INTENTIONALLY

We, the authors, will now be explicit about something that has been implied throughout. In saying something that has been unsaid, we are at risk of oversimplifying or being overly prescriptive. Please see this as an attempt to bring some ideas to your attention to support you with your own reflective practice.

The clear and ever-present purpose of this book has been to assist you to set up and adopt a process of reflective practice. Initially, our focus was on the process and how to demonstrate engagement with reflective practice. Then we made the case that it should be part of our ongoing professional practice – that it has value beyond adhering to professional expectations. At its most simple, the process requires people to identify a positive intention, determine the impact they are hoping for, and set out a plan to achieve their objective. We hope that you have had the opportunity to experience the effectiveness of this process. As we have repeatedly stated, we think that it is helpful to make Effective Reflective Practice a habit. We believe that doing so can be professionally transformative. Throughout this book, we have maintained a clear focus on professional practice. But it may have raised questions for you, as it has for us, about whether this process could apply to personal interactions as well. We believe that Effective Reflective Practice can work in personal cases too. In fact, once reflective practice becomes a habit, or a normal way of thinking, it is difficult to *avoid* using it across the broad range of interactions and relationships that are important to us. We share two personal examples below.

## Parenting: *Call of Duty*

At a busy point in my professional life, I realised that I was not as connected to my son as I would have liked. Work was encroaching into my personal time, we had a full social life and my son had different interests. I made sure to read to him at night whenever possible, but we had limited shared interests. While I did watch the latest children's cartoons and movies with him, it felt like I was doing it for him rather than being fully engaged.

I took some time out to reflect on my intention, which was to connect in a meaningful way to my son who had just become a teenager. Then I thought about what he would experience if I could make progress on this issue. I would like him to think that he and his father had something we were both passionate about. Even better, whatever this was would encourage us to spend time together and enjoy each other's company.

The plan was to identify something that he was already interested in that I could get into as well. One thing that my son enjoyed greatly was video gaming. He had been playing on consoles since he was ten years old, and he spent hours playing on games. I had played games as a child and remembered the thrill that I had experienced. I switched from being the parent who was always nagging him to get off the Playstation so that we could do something else together, and started taking an interest. I asked him to teach me how to play some of his favourite games and spent many hours of my free time developing my gaming skills. I set up my own profile and was able to play cooperatively with my son, and sometimes competitively against him.

That decision definitely strengthened the bond between us and has led to many hundreds of hours of shared gaming and game-related chat. It sustained us during the pandemic. Even today, although we live many hours apart, we will regularly get onto *Call of Duty* and play online as a duo. Not only does it give us time to chat about life in general, we give the zombies a run for their money.

## Art in Professional Settings

I have been sketching and doodling all my life. As a young boy, I could often be found spending hours at a table creating fictitious characters or maps of imaginary countries. I would be lost in what I now understand to be the state positive psychologists call 'flow'. Over the years, this interest in being visually creative has persisted and grown. When I had two children of my own and I was working in a role that took me away from home a lot, I would sketch rudimentary cartoons involving my daughter and son and leave these on the breakfast table before I left the house early in the morning as the rest of the family slept. I have also developed a reputation amongst friends and family as the creator of highly personalised funny birthday cards. Now that I have grandchildren this process has morphed into the production of collaged books depicting humorous elements about their lives.

A few years ago I became courageous enough to bring this visual creativity into my work as a coach and coach supervisor and have been continually fascinated by the impact and benefits for clients. With this in mind, I became increasingly interested in using art in reflecting on my life beyond work activities. I now intentionally set aside time each week to create an artwork and use this to explore a topic that is exciting or troubling me. Sometimes my intention is to start with a clear topic to focus on, sometimes I will start with nothing in mind and the topic will emerge from the creative process. I will then use the image I created to stimulate reflections, which in turn become the basis for insights and learning. I focus primarily on the emotions stimulated by the image and the creative process, rather than relying too much on thinking. The emotional elements are always the most powerful part of the process.

I have included an example of this process in Figures 10.1 and 10.2. In this instance my intention was to explore and strengthen the place of art in my life. A colour version of the image is included in the online materials accompanying this book. Having created the image I then explored the significance of the different elements. The light, yellow sphere in the centre on the right (1) represented for me the fascination and intrigue of engaging in visually creative activities for my own pure enjoyment. The surrounding darker, green circle shape with points (2) indicates movement and a dynamic that underlines the immense pleasure I also gain from engaging in creative activities for and with others, notably my grandchildren, family and friends. These 'others' are represented as the next three concentric rust, brown and orange rings (3) in the image. In my reflections I noticed how the colours in these rings merge and are not uniform in shape, which further suggested the dynamism, energy and connectedness of my creative endeavours.

The darkest part of the image, an incomplete brown and orange section running from the bottom left-hand corner of the image to the top right (4) introduced a more negative element into my reflections which revolved around a number of actual or potential obstacles to bringing more art creation into my life such as, for example, the availability of time and a related personal commitment to keep at it. However, the patches of purple (5) represented hope and indicated to me that, with the right motivation, I will be able to achieve that outcome.

*(Continued)*

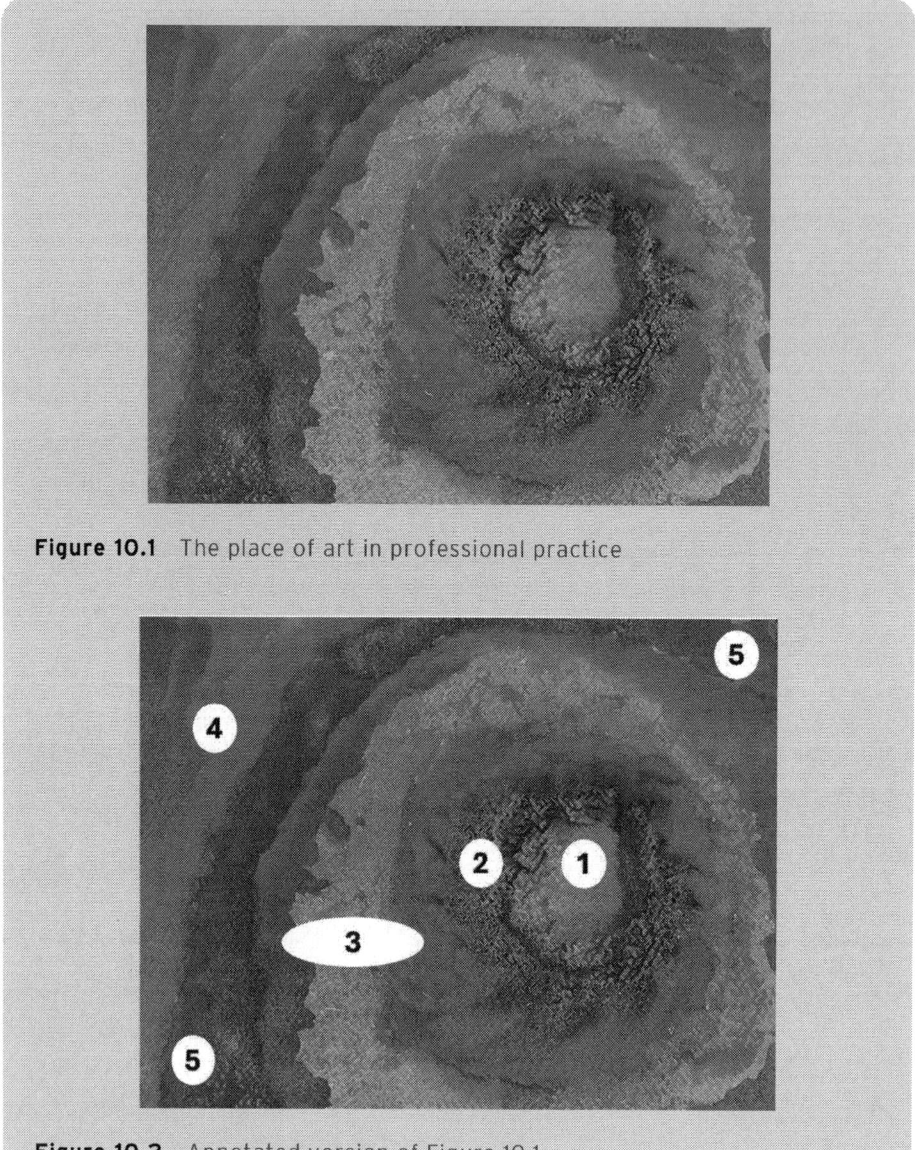


**Figure 10.1** The place of art in professional practice

**Figure 10.2** Annotated version of Figure 10.1

## SUMMARY

With time and practice, Effective Reflective Practice can become the natural way of thinking about desired change. It can positively affect our self-confidence and our self-efficacy as we realise that we have more control of our own behaviours and that we are skilled at bringing about desired change. These increases in self-confidence and self-efficacy will also impact on our in-the-moment interactions. When things go according to plan, we are more likely to note and appreciate how we have engaged in the interaction. When things fall apart, we can approach those situations with curiosity rather than despair. Knowing that we have a way of making positive changes to interactions and relationships, we are likely to bring more stability and equanimity into such situations. Effective Reflective Practice is a way of learning that has a significant impact on our way of *being*.

## Find Out More

Maurer, R. (2012). *The Spirit of Kaizen: Creating Lasting Excellence One Small Step at a Time*. New York: McGraw-Hill.

For full colour versions of all the creative drawings mentioned in this chapter, see our website: https://study.sagepub.com/nieuwerburghlove1e.

# EPILOGUE

## CHRISTIAN'S THOUGHTS ON WRITING THIS BOOK

Now that we have arrived at the end of this book, my first hope is that you, the reader, have found this journey useful. If our intentions have been met, you are now familiar with a new reflective practice framework; you have greater self-awareness about your professional practice; you are more confident when demonstrating your reflective practice in writing; and you are curious about how reflective practice can be used in other areas of your life.

I started this project optimistic about working with my co-author and friend, David Love. Once again, the process has been a wonderful learning experience. David and I have spent many hours working, reflecting, imagining and researching. So, there has been much learning. But alongside that, there has been time for extended lunches, personal reflections and discussions about life and plenty of silliness and humour.

The process of drafting, discussing, writing, re-writing, editing and re-editing has been full of joyful purpose. As we wrote, ideas started to emerge. As we edited, these ideas became clearer. And, best of all, I have learnt so much more about reflective practice. Both David and I have adopted new practices and habits as a result of what we have learnt through the process.

But have we achieved what we set out to do? We hope that we have set the ideas out clearly. We have intentionally designed a reflective practice process that is easy to capture in writing. The Effective Reflective Practice model integrates *positive intention* and pays attention to the *wellbeing* of the practitioner as well as their clients. Going beyond our original plans, we have advocated for making Effective Reflective Practice a habit, so that it can have a wider influence across your professional and personal contexts. However, the real test of the success of this book is whether it makes a difference in your life. If you feel more confident in writing *about* your reflective practice, one of our objectives will have been met. If your reflective practice leads to better outcomes for you and your clients, that is an even greater success. If you have embraced reflective practice as a way of being and interacting in the world, then our best hopes have been achieved.

## DAVID'S THOUGHTS ON WRITING THIS BOOK

When I started this book I had a number of intentions in mind:

- to explore ways of pausing to reflect
- to provide you with a core framework for creating and embedding the reflective practice habit, as well as for capturing and recording the outcomes
- to encourage you, the reader, to make your own decisions about the most effective approaches you can come up with for developing and sustaining a reflective practice habit
- to contribute to sharpening up both the 'doing' of reflective practice and the 'writing up' of reflective practice across a range of professional fields
- to encourage you to engage in serious play as a way of providing radically different lenses through which to reflect on matters of importance in your work and life
- to reflect and learn with my co-author, Christian, stretching my personal and professional thinking and capabilities in the service of others
- last but not least, to have fun in the process.

To what extent have I made these intentions a reality?

I feel satisfied that the book has covered a number of different ways to get into reflecting and developing a reflective practice habit. The core Effective Reflective Practice framework feels sufficiently structured to provide a clear foundation and also the basis for enabling professionals to record and write up their insights and learning.

The creative methods appendix (Appendix 3) includes a diverse range of approaches for bringing creativity into the mix. My hope is that this encourages you to try out and experiment with other ways of reflecting, including those methods you might at first feel uncomfortable with. Finding new ways to generate novel insights that might not otherwise emerge is the aim. I also hope the chapter on creativity encourages you to think of other ways you could bring your own particular brand of creativity into play. Again, being playful (child-like, rather than child-ish) about even the most serious of topics can enable you to make progress with seemingly insurmountable challenges.

Sticking with playfulness … I have, as anticipated, had a lot of fun writing this book with Christian. Our many meetings and conversations have been a stimulating mix of serious debate and humorous interludes, both of which have enriched our thinking and the writing process. I am also certain that I know more now about myself and about reflective practice than I did when we started on this venture. Plus, the whole experience has had positive effects on my wellbeing.

As for the impact I was seeking on reflective practice in a variety of professional settings, and beyond into people's lives … that, I feel, is for you and all the other readers to decide.

# APPENDIX 1

# TWO EXAMPLES OF EFFECTIVE REFLECTIVE PRACTICE WRITE-UPS FOR THE PURPOSES OF ASSESSMENT

## ASSIGNMENT 1: EFFECTIVE REFLECTIVE PRACTICE CYCLE: A LEADER IMPROVING BELONGING IN A TEAM

Practitioner: [name redacted]

Date: 7 June 2023

### Part 1: Brief Background and Context

#### Intention

As leader of a client-facing team whose members work independently of each other I wanted to ensure a sense of belonging, which is vital to a consistent quality of client service.

#### Motivation

- To ensure the various interdependencies work smoothly minimising the potential of clients' experiences to be undermined.

## My Values and Principles

Drawing on Schwartz' (2012) thinking, my values include:

- Benevolence – being concerned about the welfare of others, both staff and clients
- Security – seeking safety and harmony within the team
- Self-direction – encouraging team members to be self-motivated and exhibit freedom of thought and action.

## Professional Aspiration

- To be a leader who ensures colleagues experience being part of a connected team in the service of clients.

## Outcome

That team meetings are purposeful in supporting the team to do their work.

### Indicators of a Successful Outcome

- Team members are able to express their honest views about an improved sense of belonging.
- Feedback from team members about the conduct of meetings is positive.
- Client feedback indicates a high level of satisfaction with our service.

## Plan

**Table A1.1** Brief outline of plan

| What will happen? | When will it happen? | What resources are required? | Who can provide support? |
|---|---|---|---|
| I will explore the best ways to achieve belonging in a team | January 2023 | Articles, books, podcasts, conversations with colleagues | My line manager<br>Trusted team leaders |
| I will devise a new team meeting agenda to generate thinking, participation and emotional connection | January 2023 | Revised standing agenda | My line manager<br>Trusted team leaders |
| I will trial the new team meeting format focusing on team members' views of identity and belonging, and their thoughts about how these can be strengthened | February 2023 | VIA Strengths cards | Team members |

| What will happen? | When will it happen? | What resources are required? | Who can provide support? |
|---|---|---|---|
| I will create time in weekly team meetings to share how people are feeling about the work before starting on the business agenda | February 2023 | Allocated time | Team members |
| I will re-orientate the team meeting as a collaborative and creative idea-generating forum | January to April | Thinking Environment principles & practices | Team members |
| I will designate a team meeting as a vehicle for reviewing progress towards the outcome | June 2023 | None | Team members |

As part of the planning process, I undertook an ethical review and an Equality Impact Assessment. The latter took into account the different levels of experience and expertise, and the diverse composition of the team in terms of ethnic origin and gender. I was determined not to make any assumptions about individuals and wanted to work with colleagues to find ways to develop stronger connections across the team. My ethical review included links to these considerations in that I was keen to be alert to the cultural sensitivities discussions about belonging might invoke. In addition I revisited the ethical standards in our professional field to remind myself of these expectations.

## Hypotheses

Hypothesis 1: If team meetings allow space for colleagues to express how they are feeling currently about their work, they will be able to offload the stress they experience and not allow this to interfere with their client relationships.

Hypothesis 2: If I encourage the establishment of a 'thinking environment' (Kline, 2002), in meetings, then opportunities will be created for team members to explore and influence how they work, become more engaged and generate ideas for improving the client experience.

## Experimentation

### What Worked Well

- The engagement of some team members with the discussion about the three key components of belonging: comfort, connection and contribution (Deloitte, 2020).
- My use of the Values-in-Action (VIA) Strengths cards to identify individual and collective strengths.
- My introduction of a 'thinking environment' to explore work-related topics in depth.

### What Worked Less Well

- Some team members were reluctant to discuss belonging.
- Team members were uncomfortable sharing their emotions.

### Results

Team members:

- Began to share their emotions and the impact on their work (Hypothesis 1 supported)
- Became convinced of the need to shift to a more collaborative culture (Hypothesis 2 supported).

# Part 2: Reflections and Learning

## Appraisal

Overall, this reflective practice cycle was successful. While it has taken much longer to achieve the desired outcome than I originally envisaged my intended outcome was achieved.

## Desired Outcome for the Team and Clients

The sense of belonging in the team has strengthened. This has been demonstrated through:

- Increased engagement by all team members in meetings – with people feeling able to raise potentially sensitive issues related, for example to knowledge backgrounds, race, gender and neurotype
- A team culture that is beginning to embody continual creative ideas generation for ways to improve our service
- An enhanced collective pride in the team's achievements.

Our clients are noticing a difference too. Our latest client satisfaction survey shows significantly improved results and team members are actively seeking verbal feedback from clients in their interactions.

Colleagues we interact with in our organisation have also commented on the improved effectiveness and cohesion of our team.

## My Intention

My intention, as leader of the team, was to create the conditions that would enable team members to have a strong and genuine sense of belonging. I believe I achieved this intention and have a great deal of satisfaction that the team now sees a more collaborative approach as the norm.

## My Learning and Reflections

### My Motivation

I was very motivated by my original intention. In setting my intention I confirmed to myself that people finding meaning and a strong connection to their work is extremely important to me. This also underlined how important it is for me to feel my own contribution is meaningful and purposeful. I feel my intention was very closely aligned to my values.

My learning preference is strongly reflective and my MBTI (Rogers, 2007) type (INFJ) means I approach work-related issues in a thoughtful, people-oriented way. I have a tendency to need time and space to think things through before making a response. I noticed that I was not responsive enough in-the-moment in some team meetings to work with the expressed concerns of some team members about revealing sensitive information about themselves. Emotionally, the experience was a bit of a rollercoaster – I sometimes felt frustrated by the lack of progress, while at other times exhilarated by the significant personal shifts I could see happening across the team, with corresponding impacts on my motivation.

### My Outcome

I over-estimated how straightforward it would be to achieve my desired outcome. While I had anticipated some reluctance on the part of the team, I underestimated how long it would take for them to see the benefits I could see.

With hindsight my outcome was rather ambitious, particularly in the timescale I envisaged, and it might have been better to break this down into more manageable 'chunks'. For example, I could have focused on one of the factors affecting belonging rather than all three at once. On the other hand, those factors are interrelated and a more holistic approach replicated reality more accurately.

## My Plan

As stated above I think my plan may have been ambitious – certainly in terms of timescale. Some aspects of the plan worked well. For example, I was able to initiate a discussion with the team about belonging, albeit with some important setbacks primarily related to a reluctance of some colleagues to engage fully.

I have learnt that I can be tenacious and determined in the face of opposition and by persevering with a strong values-based intention I can achieve outcomes. I noticed with time to stand back and engage in further reflection, I could return to the fray with a revised approach, which would prove fruitful. For example, switching the focus on the strengths activity to begin with the whole team's capabilities rather than those of individuals, created the conditions for the latter to then be explored.

I learnt that my top three Values-in-Action (VIA) Strengths are creativity/adaptability, honesty/authenticity and appreciation of beauty/admiration. I was able to deploy these strengths to create openness and find a variety of interesting ways to encourage the team to engage.

The challenges I encountered from some members of the team about the risks related to them revealing their views and opinions created an ethical dilemma for me. My ethical review alerted me to the extent to which we can expect team members to be fully authentic in bringing their whole selves to work. I began to wonder to what extent workplaces and leaders can really expect colleagues to 'give their all' to the work. There is an expectation that we bring all of ourselves authentically to our roles – but I noticed my own personal discomfort and limits with opening up about my values and beliefs. I think recognising this in myself helped me be realistic about how much I could expect team members to engage more openly and my genuine honesty about this created the conditions that allowed others to be in control of what they revealed.

I learnt that I am able to work sensitively and with integrity, which was commented on positively by several members of the team. I discovered that I am a good listener, which I now realise is an important skill for creating strong working relationships. In line with my MBTI type I am not comfortable being forthright with constructive criticism of others. In a more open and collaborative team culture I will need to develop this ability as another way in to handling resistance. As an INFJ I also need to be alert to the possibility that I may come across as knowing what's best for people and that I can have a tendency towards perfectionism. This may distort my opinion of others' performance and further exacerbate a slow transition from reflection to action.

Further, the Equality Impact Assessment I undertook as part of my planning underlined the importance of taking steps to make sure everyone, regardless of background, can express their views and be properly heard in order that they can contribute to improving communication and client experiences. I work with a diverse team serving a very diverse population. My experiments confirmed to me that the team's diversity is a rich source of experience and learning that enables us to respond effectively to the wide range of needs and aspirations in the community. I discovered that a member of our team, who is always extremely active, is neuro-divergent and I learnt ways of adapting my approach (by ensuring all four learning styles are always in play) so as not to disadvantage them in encouraging a more reflective approach to team working.

If I was doing this again I would break down the outcome into stages and allow more time for implementation. On the one hand my preference for reflection can mean I hold back from action, on the other, once I have come to a conclusion about a way forward I can be impatient to make it happen.

## My Experiments

The most important learning I took away from the experimentation phase was that I can be very creative in designing ways to enable colleagues to engage with potentially sensitive issues. An example of this is the way I drew on the Time To Think (Kline, 2002) process to encourage ideas generation and my use of the VIA Strengths picture cards to stimulate a discussion.

I learnt that it can take time and effort for colleagues to feel comfortable with new ways of doing things. I need to acknowledge more intentionally that I, as a reflector, will have spent time thinking through the implications of a new idea and others will need that space too.

Overall, I think my planned experiments went well, although I think I could have been clearer about my intentions when introducing each one. Again, my tendency towards reflection can mean I do not always fully communicate the rationales for my suggestions or decisions clearly to others, meaning colleagues cannot see the thinking that led to a particular conclusion. If I am determined to create more openness in team discussions, I must reveal more of how I have arrived at a position and put this up for scrutiny by the team.

In planning my experiments I used the four learning styles to test my approach. As a strong reflector I can readily stand back and give detailed thought to a topic. However, this can lead to procrastination fuelled by a desire to have 'all the data' before making a move. For example, I intentionally viewed my plan through the activist lens to check that my plan would lead to action towards an outcome.

## My Conclusions

I learnt a great deal about belonging in teams. Firstly, people need to feel comfortable at work (i.e. they need to experience being treated fairly and with respect by everyone) (Deloitte, 2020). I realise that this is an ongoing dilemma to be managed, rather than a problem with a one-off solution.

Secondly, team members need to feel connected to each other, which includes being able to speak up and express ideas and emotions. I have learnt that individuals can have widely different attitudes to risk-taking in relation to speaking up in the workplace. There can be a considerable gulf between a simple statement that it's OK to 'speak truth to power' and feeling that it is safe to do so. I believe I have strengthened my ability to work constructively with uncertainty in such sensitive arenas and, over time, to role model behaviours which demonstrate a genuine commitment to seeking and accepting constructive criticism.

Thirdly, people need to feel they are contributing to meaningful work outcomes. They need to see how their unique strengths help the team achieve outcomes for the organisation and clients. One of the major successes of this reflective cycle has been my capacity to design and implement team activities that focus firmly on our diverse, and collective, strengths.

With sufficient preparation I now know that I can manage difficult situations effectively. Having worked through several initial instances of powerful negative responses from some team members I need to be more confident about my capabilities and allay my anxieties about dealing with conflict and resistance. In addition, I have learnt that engaging the team in exploring how conflict can arise, rather than seeing myself as solely responsible for team harmony, creates greater collective understanding. This in turn leads to the team generating and as a result, taking greater ownership of the ideas for removing or minimising tensions.

One source of team members' negativity related to the difficulties caused by other teams in our organisation when they do not perform satisfactorily. In those circumstances my team finds itself compensating for gaps in the service in order that clients are not affected. This issue requires further exploration.

A further learning point is that the introduction and use of creative approaches (such as the VIA Strengths cards) can enable sensitive issues to be explored because they place those issues at one removed from the individuals involved. Focusing people's attention on the cards meant that team members were not engaged in direct eye contact with each other all the way through a conversation about strengths with the result that they could be more open.

I have strong working and personal relationships with other team leaders at my level in the organisation. I chose to 'buddy up' with one of these colleagues to share the progress of my plan. She was extremely helpful in acting as a sounding board for my thinking, especially when I was facing challenges. I noticed that in addition to my reflector capabilities talking things through with a partner was invaluable in crystallising what to try next. This experience has boosted my confidence as a leader and I will continue this relationship and build others with similarly trusted colleagues across the organisation, which I now see could benefit other teams in my organisation. As an INFJ I can neglect to approach others when I need help. This experience has reminded me that when I reach out for support it is available and produces benefits.

Contrary to my initial perceptions of myself I can see now that I can be quietly influential of others in ways which acknowledge them as human beings and take on board their concerns and ideas. I feel more comfortable seeking feedback about my behaviours from colleagues as well as instigating occasional conversations with clients to gain their views about our service.

I feel much more aware of my capabilities as a leader and of the areas I need to focus my development. I propose to make the following improvements to my practice. I will:

- Develop my listening, facilitation and coaching skills so that I am better able to manage team meetings in collaborative ways
- Strengthen my skills in political astuteness so that I am better equipped to manage the intricacies of team dynamics
- Be at ease with 'good enough' rather than perfection
- Create more time for one-to-one meetings with team members to establish an additional avenue for them to raise concerns and explore their thinking and ideas with me
- Devise a plan with my own manager which focuses on sustaining the emerging, new team culture I have initiated
- Explore constructively with my fellow managers (and my line manager) the systemic issues impacting the connections between teams so that the pressures felt by team members are minimised
- Try to take myself a little less seriously.

I will test the effectiveness of these actions by instigating regular conversations about their impact with team members, team leader colleagues, my line manager and clients.

Overall I have learnt that I am a compassionate and creative human being who places the wellbeing of people at the heart of how I relate to others.

## References

Deloitte (2020). *Deloitte Insights: The Social Enterprise at Work – Paradox as a Path Forward*. Deloitte Global Human Capital Trends.

Kline, N. (2002). *Time to think. Listening to ignite the human mind*. London: Cassell.

Rogers, J. (2007). *Sixteen Personality Types – At Work in Organisations*. London: Management Futures Ltd.

Schwartz, S. H. (2012). An overview of the Schwartz theory of basic values. *Online Readings in Psychology and Culture, 2*(1).

# ASSIGNMENT 2: EFFECTIVE REFLECTIVE PRACTICE CYCLE: FACILITATION OF WORKSHOPS

Practitioner: [name redacted]

Date: 4 June 2023

## Part 1: What Happened?

### Intention

To enhance my facilitation practice during workshops by connecting with individual participants.

### Motivation

- To have a meaningful impact on workshop participants and for the learning opportunity to be as effective as possible.

### My Values and Principles

- I like to see people achieve more of their potential.
- I believe that it is important to create positive learning environments.
- One of my strengths is 'love of learning.'

### Professional Aspirations

- To be seen as one of those educators that can have a positive and meaningful long-term impact on learners.
- To support the learning of people in a way that is empowering and allows them to feel valued.

### Outcome

That workshop participants will feel valued by having an opportunity for one-to-one interaction with me as a facilitator.

#### Indicators of a Successful Outcome

- Participants will evaluate the workshop positively.
- Evaluations will include some references to the impact of my facilitation style.
- Positive verbal feedback during the workshops.

## Plan

**Table A1.2** Brief outline of plan

| What will happen? | When it will happen? | What resources are needed? | Who can provide support? |
|---|---|---|---|
| I will review literature (e.g. Burke & Passmore, 2019) and podcasts on the use of strengths during workshops | April and May 2023 | Articles, books, podcasts | Co-facilitator of workshop; peers who are also facilitators; experts in positive psychology and strengths use |
| Introduce new activity during workshop: Identify participants' strengths and record these in order to share individually at the end of the workshop | 1-3 June 2023 | Strengths cards, time for the activity. | Will need to discuss with co-facilitator of the workshop and the course administrator who has agreed the outline of the workshop. |
| Seek feedback from participants and co-facilitator | 3 June 2023 | Time on the day. | Workshop participants and co-facilitator. |
| Read evaluation forms | June/July 2023 | Access to evaluation forms. | Course administrator. |

As part of the planning process, I undertook an ethical review and an Equality Impact Assessment. The ethical review highlighted the risk of providing some people with much more value than others, and the EIA alerted me to the potential of inadvertent discrimination because people from some cultural contexts might be less likely to take up an offer of additional 1-1 interaction.

## Hypotheses

- Hypothesis 1: The majority of participants will want to hear about their strengths from me.
- Hypothesis 2: There will be positive verbal feedback from participants after I have told them the strength that I have observed in them.

## Experimentation

### What Worked Well

- Participants were enthusiastic about receiving feedback from me.
- A few participants expressed their gratitude for the opportunity.
- A few participants said that they felt valued and appreciated.
- The co-facilitator provided very positive feedback about the activity.
- I enjoyed the activity.

### What did not Work

- Those participants that had to leave early did not have an opportunity to receive feedback from me.
- There was no agreed 'queuing' system for participants who wanted to receive feedback from me at the end of the workshop.

### Results

- Most participants did stay on after the workshop to receive feedback from me. (Hypothesis 1 supported)
- Many participants provided positive feedback about the exercise. (Hypothesis 2 supported)

## Part 2: What did I Learn?

### Appraisal

Overall, the reflective practice cycle was successful.

### Desired Outcome for the Client

That workshop participants did feel valued by having an opportunity for one-to-one interaction with me as a facilitator. This was despite the fact that the activity did not go as smoothly as I had imagined. I will need to reflect further and have discussions with my co-facilitator to make some further tweaks to the activity. I felt very positive when participants were queuing up to talk to me. I was also very grateful to receive positive comments from the participants. One of them said 'I really appreciated the way that you got to know each of us. It really made this a very meaningful learning experience for me'.

### My Intention

My intention was to enhance my facilitation practice by connecting with individual participants. I felt that I achieved this intention and I think that it had the effect that I was hoping it would have.

### My Learning and Reflections

#### Motivation and Intention

I was highly motivated to undertake this reflective practice cycle. I realised that my commitment to this work goes beyond simply 'doing a good job' or 'being a competent professional'. It is important for me to feel that I have had a positive impact on the learning of workshop participants. This intention was very closely aligned to my values and the kind of educator that I would like to be – making it feel like quite a 'high stakes' experiment.

Even though I was very clear about my intention, I have realised that I was still unsure whether this strategy would work well with this particular group. My concern was that everyone would want to get away quickly at the end of a three-day workshop, especially as it ended on a Saturday afternoon. Even though I talked this through with colleagues, I need to try things out and experience success before I can adopt new facilitation practices.

One of my strengths is 'love of learning' (Peterson & Seligman, 2004) and that has been helpful in a number of ways. First, I brought a genuinely curious mindset to this cycle and was very keen to learn about better ways of facilitating. Second, the outcome related to supporting the learning of others. I tend to learn best when I see things happening in practice, so I enjoyed the opportunity to try this out. Having experienced it, I'm now more convinced that this is a good idea, even though I already have further ideas about how to improve the activity for the next workshop.

## Outcome

Although the outcome was achieved, I have realised that there is a risk of allocating too much time for this activity. My desire to make sure that participants feel valued can lead me to over-rating the importance of this intervention. My co-facilitator and I have spoken before about our perceptions that there is so much content that we are trying to squeeze into three days. I plan to keep the activity, but make it more efficient in future workshops.

Another thought that I captured in my reflective journal on the second day of the workshop was 'my interactions with the participants should be conveying that I value them throughout the three days of the workshop. I should not have to rely entirely on one activity that takes place on the third day of the workshop to convey to participants that I value them. The activity is simply an additional indicator of this. Its purpose is to ensure that everyone has the opportunity to have a one-to-one interaction with me – but this does not mean that it is the *only* opportunity.'

## The Plan

Reading up on the use of strengths and the impact it can have on people when their strengths are recognised and acknowledged (Niemic, 2018) was very helpful for me. So, the development of the plan was relatively straightforward. But what I learnt about myself is that I remain doubtful about new interventions until I have seen them happening in real situations. Talking to my co-facilitator about the idea was more reassuring since he was experienced with working with similar groups. His input was important to me in writing up the plan. Nonetheless, I was still not 100% confident until we tried it out. I want to do some more thinking about this. On the one hand, I think it's good that I had the courage to try it out anyway, even though I was not sure whether it would work. On the other, there's a risk that I get stuck in my ways because I won't try things out until I'm sure they will work. When I think about this, I'm starting to understand that I need to try things out in real-life situations—but I will only try things out if there is already a good chance that it will work. This could mean that I do not go for really innovative or creative strategies. Maybe I'm a little bit too risk averse because getting it right is so important for me?

I did not identify any particular ethical issues when reviewing my plan. However, I made some adaptations after undertaking an Equality Impact Assessment. With reflection, I wondered whether everyone would be confident enough to come up to me to ask for feedback? Might some people feel intimidated to do so? Would some people prefer written feedback instead? Would some people have to leave earlier than the end because of other commitments? After considering these questions, I broadened the activity so that participants could ask for in-person feedback or ask for it to be sent via email.

## The Experiment

The most important learning I took from the experimentation stage is the need to be quite explicit about how the activity will take place. The experiment made me realise that this activity needs to be very clearly defined because it seemed to straddle the clear ending of the formal workshop. In other words, it started before the formal 'end time' of 4:00pm but did not conclude until about 4:10pm. So, it can impact the experience of how the three-day workshop ends. Greater clarity from me about how much time the activity will take and a clearer explanation to everyone about the logistics of the last 30 minutes will be important in future.

What I have learnt about myself is that I can get too focused on one element of the workshop, so I need to see any new activities as complementing everything else that is already in place. Putting too much emphasis on one component of a three-day workshop could lead me to undermining my original intention which was to ensure that participants feel valued.

What I have learnt about my clients is that they appreciate the care and attention that I provide throughout the three-day workshop, and that the last activity is almost like the 'icing on the cake'. I noticed that the participants left the workshop in very high spirits. Compared to the last time I co-facilitated this workshop, the last hour was very high-energy and positive.

I will need to take into account a few systemic factors as I continue to refine this new approach. First, adding any activity means that there is less time for something else. Before the next workshop, my co-facilitator and I will review the entire curriculum to ensure that we cover all the learning outcomes that have been advertised to participants. Second, finishing the workshop on a Saturday means that many participants are keen to finish early in order to return to loved ones. That is another reason that the ending of the workshop should be as tight and focused as possible.

The best learning from the experiment is that the participants found the new activity very meaningful and that I enjoyed it too. I have to be careful that this activity is not just about me ending the workshop on a positive note. One thing that I had not taken into account is that both my co-facilitator and I were relatively tired by the end of facilitating a three-day workshop. This experiment has provided us with a high-impact close to the workshop that taps into the positive energy of the participants as well as the facilitators. We both left the session feeling positive and uplifted.

## Conclusions

I've learnt that it is helpful to try new ideas and initiatives—and that I get a lot out of talking to colleagues about this. They give me greater confidence to try out new things. This cycle of reflective practice has highlighted to me how important being an inspiring facilitator is to me. Creating effective environments for learning is what I would like to do—and I will continue to ask questions about how I can do it better.

This cycle has boosted my confidence to try out new ideas and take some risks in the pursuit of inspiring outcomes for learners. I am excited about the idea of supporting learners to have meaningful and memorable experiences through the workshops that I deliver. And this way of doing it builds on my natural preference to focus on positives and strengths, so it feels like an authentic way forward.

Taking a broader view, I will look for situations where I can acknowledge and appreciate people individually. I am also keen to be similarly intentional about all my professional interactions as well as personal ones.

# References

Burke, J. & Passmore, J. (2019). Strengths based coaching: A positive psychology intervention, in L. Van Zyl & S. Rothmann Sr. (Eds). *Theoretical Approaches to Multi-Cultural Positive Psychological Interventions (pp. 463 -75)*. New York: Springer.

Niemiec, R. M. (2018). *Character Strengths Interventions: A Field-guide for Practitioners*. Boston: Hogrefe.

Peterson, C. & Seligman, M. (2004). *Character Strengths and Virtues: A Handbook and Classification*. Oxford: Oxford University Press.

# APPENDIX 2

## DEMONSTRATING REFLECTIVE PRACTICE THROUGH ACADEMIC WRITING: INDICATIVE MARKING OF ASSIGNMENTS 1 AND 2

This appendix uses the Effective Reflective Practice Marking Guide to provide an indicative assessment of the two sample assignments from Appendix 1.

**Table A2.1** Indicative marking of assignment 1

**Note: Italicised text indicates the assessor's mark; bold italicised text highlights aspects that would enable a Distinction to be awarded.**

**OVERALL MARK: (A very good) MERIT**

| | Fail [Refer] [F] | Good [Pass] [C] | *Very Good [Merit] [B]* | Excellent [Distinction] [A] |
|---|---|---|---|---|
| **Clarity of purpose** | Purpose of the reflective practice is not clear | The desired outcome of the reflective practice is clearly presented | Clear statement of the desired outcome and an explanation of what led to the cycle of reflective practice | *Clear, engaging presentation of the desired outcome. Explanation of the positive intention that initiated the cycle of reflective practice. A discussion of what would be different for clients.* |
| **Relevance of action plan** | No action plan, or a plan that does not seem appropriate for the desired outcome. No reflections on the impact of the plan on others. | A well-designed action plan is presented. Ethics is mentioned and there is a consideration of the impact of the plan on others. | *A well-designed action plan is presented briefly and with clarity. There is a direct link to the desired outcome and the positive intention. There is a thoughtful exploration of the ethical implications and the impact of the plan on others is carefully considered.* | A well-designed action plan is presented briefly and with clarity. There is a direct link to the desired outcome. ***There are references to theories or research that inform the design of the plan.*** There is a thoughtful exploration of the ethical implications and the impact of the plan on others is carefully considered. ***An equality impact assessment review is included as an appendix.*** |
| **Evidence of new learning** | Process is described but there is little or no evidence of new learning | There are few examples of new learning | Learning points are clearly presented. There is evidence of new learning and insights. | *New learning is set out explicitly. Insights are shared throughout the reflective writing. The implications of the new learning on professional practice are explained.* |
| **Self-awareness** | Little or no evidence of self-awareness. No reference to wellbeing. Values and principles not discussed. | Some evidence of self-awareness. Wellbeing is mentioned. Personal integrity is discussed. | Good evidence of self-awareness with discussion about personal preferences. Attention is paid to wellbeing. Personal values and principles are explored. | *Evidence of high levels of self-awareness with discussion of personal preferences and an understanding of motivation. Wellbeing is a priority. Personal values and principles are thoughtfully presented.* |
| **Depth of reflections and analysis** | Text is mostly descriptive with little analysis | Text combines both description and analysis. Occasional reference to theories or research. | *Evidence of professional curiosity. Text goes beyond surface level descriptions to explore deeper meaning. Most of the text focuses on reflection and analysis. Some references to relevant theories or research.* | Evidence of professional curiosity. Text focuses on reflection and analysis. There are deep and insightful reflections throughout. ***The analysis includes discussion of relevant theories or recent research studies.*** |
| **Thoughts and emotions** | No discussion of thoughts or emotions | Some discussion of both thoughts and emotions | *Good balance of discussion about thoughts and emotions. Evidence of ongoing exploration of the relationship between the two.* | Excellent commentary on the thoughts and emotions experienced during the cycle of reflective practice. ***Excerpt from reflective journal that shows consideration of thoughts and emotions provided as an appendix.*** |
| **Authentic and honest** | No evidence of honest reflections | Some honest comments about thoughts or emotions | Evidence of vulnerability and openness when reflecting on learning and professional impact | *Evidence of vulnerability and openness when reflecting on learning and professional impact. Includes honest appraisal of professional practice.* |

**Table A2.2** Indicative marking of assignment 2

**Note: Italicised text indicates the assessor's mark; bold italicised text highlights aspects that would enable a Distinction to be awarded.**
**OVERALL MARK: (A very good) MERIT**

| | Fail [Refer] [F] | Good [Pass] [C] | *Very Good [Merit] [B]* | Excellent [Distinction] [A] |
|---|---|---|---|---|
| **Clarity of purpose** | Purpose of the reflective practice is not clear | The desired outcome of the reflective practice is clearly presented | Clear statement of the desired outcome and an explanation of what led to the cycle of reflective practice | *Clear, engaging presentation of the desired outcome. Explanation of the positive intention that initiated the cycle of reflective practice. A discussion of what would be different for clients.* |
| **Relevance of action plan** | No action plan, or a plan that does not seem appropriate for the desired outcome. No reflections on the impact of the plan on others. | A well-designed action plan is presented. Ethics is mentioned and there is a consideration of the impact of the plan on others. | *A well-designed action plan is presented briefly and with clarity. There is a direct link to the desired outcome and the positive intention. There is a thoughtful exploration of the ethical implications and the impact of the plan on others is carefully considered.* | A well-designed action plan is presented briefly and with clarity. There is a direct link to the desired outcome. There are references to theories or research that inform the design of the plan. There is a thoughtful exploration of the ethical implications and the impact of the plan on others is carefully considered. ***An equality impact assessment review is included as an appendix.*** |
| **Evidence of new learning** | Process is described but there is little or no evidence of new learning | There are few examples of new learning | Learning points are clearly presented. There is evidence of new learning and insights. | *New learning is set out explicitly. Insights are shared throughout the reflective writing. The implications of the new learning on professional practice are explained.* |
| **Self-awareness** | Little or no evidence of self-awareness. No reference to wellbeing. Values and principles not discussed. | Some evidence of self-awareness. Wellbeing is mentioned. Personal integrity is discussed. | *Good evidence of self-awareness with discussion about personal preferences. Attention is paid to wellbeing. Personal values and principles are explored.* | Evidence of high levels of self-awareness with discussion of personal preferences and an understanding of motivation. ***Wellbeing is a priority.*** Personal values and principles are thoughtfully presented. |
| **Depth of reflections and analysis** | Text is mostly descriptive with little analysis | Text combines both description and analysis. Occasional reference to theories or research. | *Evidence of professional curiosity. Text goes beyond surface level descriptions to explore deeper meaning. Most of the text focuses on reflection and analysis. Some references to relevant theories or research.* | Evidence of professional curiosity. Text focuses on reflection and analysis. There are deep and insightful reflections throughout. ***The analysis includes discussion of relevant theories or recent research studies.*** |
| **Thoughts and emotions** | No discussion of thoughts or emotions | Some discussion of both thoughts and emotions | *Good balance of discussion about thoughts and emotions. Evidence of ongoing exploration of the relationship between the two.* | Excellent commentary on the thoughts and emotions experienced during the cycle of reflective practice. ***Excerpt from reflective journal that shows consideration of thoughts and emotions provided as an appendix.*** |
| **Authentic and honest** | No evidence of honest reflections | Some honest comments about thoughts or emotions | Evidence of vulnerability and openness when reflecting on learning and professional impact | *Evidence of vulnerability and openness when reflecting on learning and professional impact. Includes honest appraisal of professional practice.* |

# APPENDIX 3
# A SELECTION OF CREATIVE REFLECTIVE METHODS

## INTRODUCTION

There are many methods that can be used to find new and different ways of reflecting by tapping into your creativity. Such methods can be very helpful as part of a structured reflective practice process. This is especially relevant when exploring complicated or difficult topics where the traditional logical, rational and analytical thinking processes may not be producing insights. Creativity can also be used to generate insights from your achievements and successes.

This appendix takes you through various creative methods for reflecting on your practice and is an accompaniment to Chapter 9: 'Creativity in reflective practice'. As we suggest in that chapter it may be a helpful part of your reflective practice to note which ones you feel drawn to – and which you are less open to. What are your reasons for these reactions? What might that tell you about your preferences for ways of learning? What implications might there be for your relationships with clients and colleagues? If you have a special interest or talent in one of these methods (like writing poetry, for instance), see what happens when you apply this in your reflective activities. Throughout this book we have been encouraging you to find balance between staying close to your comfort zone and venturing beyond it. Staying in your comfort zone risks complacency while moving too far away from it can lead to discomfort. However, discomfort is what might provide you with new insights and a different perspective through which to create and view your reflections. There is no need for you to be proficient in the methods you decide to use.

The list of approaches included here is by no means exhaustive. Networking with other reflective practitioners and searches on the internet will generate a wealth of other possibilities. We encourage you to continually try out ways of reflecting creatively that you have not yet experienced to see how they work for you. We also wholeheartedly encourage you to design your own reflective processes based on the creative interests and passions in your work and life.

Table A3.1 gives an indication of the key purposes of each creative method and provides an indication of the time you might need to set aside to use it effectively. It is worth remembering:

- All the methods can be used for exploring situations, opening up possibilities, expanding perspectives and generating insights (i.e. they encourage divergent thinking)
- Some methods also have elements of convergent thinking (where decisions are made about closing down the options and deciding the best possible ways forward); these are particularly useful for planning and outcome-setting purposes in reflective practice
- All the methods have a number of possible uses; Table A3.1 suggests the most likely purpose for choosing particular methods but you may decide to use them in different ways to meet your requirements
- Some methods can be used quite quickly, others demand a greater investment of time; you may be able to find helpful ways of using them over different timescales to those indicated in the table
- The methods outlined here are just part of the possible ways you can 'go deeper'; what others do you already know? Think creatively about how you might use your particular talents and strengths to come up with your own ways of exploring and reflecting more deeply.

**Table A3.1** Methods for generating insights

| | Method | Purpose |
|---|---|---|
| **Methods for generating insights**<br>**Time involved: up to 30 minutes** | | |
| 1 | Seeing through other people's eyes | Gaining new perspectives |
| 2 | Doodling | Exploring possibilities |
| 3 | Mindfulness | Gaining new perspectives |
| 4 | Visualisation | Setting outcomes |
| 5 | Mindmapping | Exploring<br>Reviewing<br>Planning |
| 6 | Ask a chatbot | Gaining new perspectives |
| 7 | Elevator pitch | Setting goals |
| **Methods for generating insights**<br>**Time involved: 30–60 minutes** | | |
| | **Method** | **Purpose** |
| 8 | Using visual images | Overcoming stuckness |
| 9 | Reflecting on relationships | Exploring relationships<br>organisational contexts and systems |

| Methods for generating insights<br>Time involved: 30–60 minutes | | |
|---|---|---|
| 10 | Sketching | Overcoming stuckness<br>Surfacing emotions |
| 11 | Reading poetry | Surfacing emotions |
| 12 | Writing poetry | Surfacing emotions |
| 13 | Modelling | Exploring relationships, organisational contexts and systems |
| 14 | Mindfulness – Walking meditation | Gaining new perspectives |
| 15 | Mindfulness – Body scan | Gaining new perspectives |
| 16 | Email from someone important | Gaining new perspectives |
| 17 | Listen to yourself better | Gaining new perspectives |

| Methods for generating insights<br>Time involved: 60+ minutes | | |
|---|---|---|
| | **Method** | **Purpose** |
| 18 | Storytelling | Gaining new perspectives |
| 19 | Constellations | Exploring relationships, organisational contexts and systems |
| 20 | Storyboarding | Planning |
| 21 | Cartoons | Gaining new perspectives |

### Find Out More

Lucas, M. (2023). *Creating the Reflective Habit: A Practical Guide for Coaches, Mentors and Leaders*. Abingdon: Routledge.

# METHODS REQUIRING UP TO 30 MINUTES

## Seeing through Other People's Eyes

All the methods shared in this chapter involve looking at something from different perspectives. A simple way to achieve this is to imagine viewing your topic through someone else's eyes.

### How to Use this Method

1 Imagine someone else exploring the same questions that you are thinking about. This involves imagining how your chosen person would approach the same situation. Examples include: someone you know and admire who deals with similar situations well; someone who you think of as a little bit 'quirky'; a famous personality – such as the manager of your favourite sports team, a popular musician, a contemporary politician or a figure from history.

2 Make a list of all the ways your chosen person might and act in the situation. Which of these might inform how you hope to tackle what you are exploring?

It is also worth considering why you believe this person would think and act in these ways. What does your answer suggest about the values you have assumed underpin their supposed decisions? How do these values fit with the values you wish to see demonstrated in your own thinking and actions?

## Doodling

Working with scribbles and doodles is a form of reflection that is engaging, easy to use and insightful.

### You Will Need

- Felt-tipped pens, pencils and/or crayons in a variety of colours.
- Sheets of plain paper (A4 or A3).

### How to Use this Method

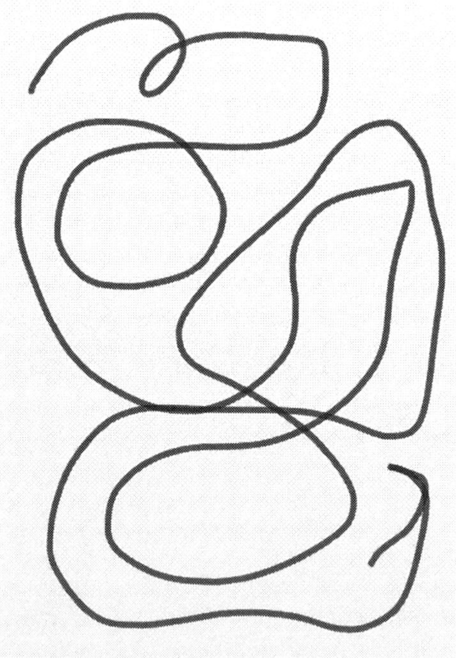

**Figure A3.1** Initial Doodle

1 Start from the intention for your reflection – a question or topic.
2 Create a random doodle or scribble – keep this as simple as possible.
3 Look closely at your doodle:

- What do you see?
- How might that connect to your reflective intention?

4 Turn your doodle 90 degrees so that it is on its side.

**Figure A3.2** Doodle rotated 90 degrees

- What do you see now?
- How might that connect to your reflective intention?

5 Rotate your doodle another 90 degrees so that it is upside down.

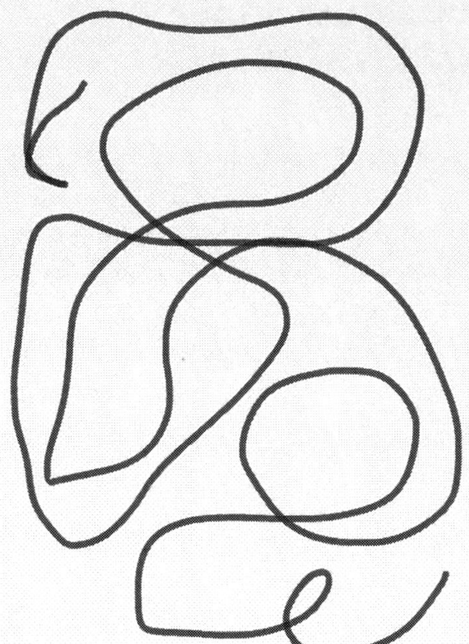

**Figure A3.3** Doodle rotated 180 degrees

- What do you see now?
- How might that connect to your topic of focus?

6 Rotate your doodle another 90 degrees.

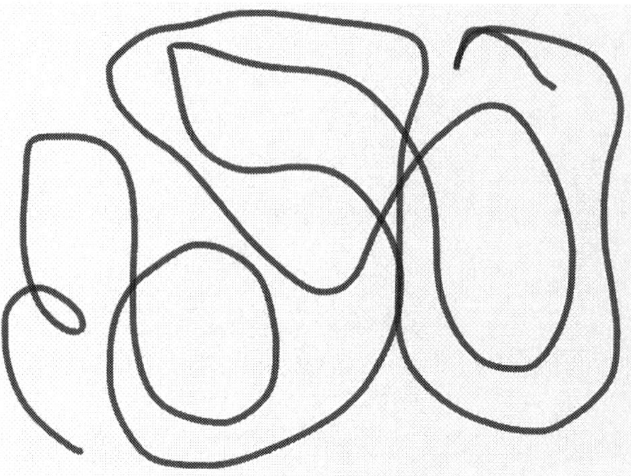

**Figure A3.4** Doodle rotated 270 degrees

- Now what do you see?
- How might that connect to your reflective intention?

7 Review all the connections you have made over the four orientations and explore the implications for your reflective topic. What insights have you gained? How will these insights help you?

## Alternative Approach

Having created your doodle choose one of the four orientations. From this viewpoint does the doodle suggest a new image to you? Be creative with your doodle, bringing the image alive on the page. This might involve adding features using extra marks, lines or shapes, thickening existing lines and/or colouring in sections to make the image more prominent. You could also add two or three words that come to mind about the image.

**Figure A3.5** Original doodle

**entangled struggling**

**Figure A3.6** Annotated image suggested by original doodle

- How might this image connect to your reflective topic?

*Scribbles by David. With thanks to Pauline Esson who facilitated a session about scribble coaching at an Art-based Practitioners' Forum in February 2023.*

### Find Out More

Search on YouTube for *Shelley Klammer*, who demonstrates her approach to using scribbling in her work.

## Mindfulness

Mindfulness has well-researched benefits for health and wellbeing. There is also evidence to suggest that mindfulness can aid more flexible thinking and clarity, which has obvious positive implications for reflective practice. Mindfulness practice involves becoming more adept at noticing your thoughts and setting them aside without forming judgements about them.

Practising mindfulness can take simple forms, including:

- *Paying attention:* slowing down in order to become more aware of and notice what is going on around you, experiencing your immediate environment with all of your senses – touch, sound, sight, smell and taste
- *Living in the moment:* cultivating an intention to be open, accepting, and find pleasure in all your activities
- *Accepting yourself:* behaving towards yourself as you would a loved one
- *Focusing on your breathing:* paying attention for a short period of time to your breathing as it enters and leaves your body, resulting in you becoming calm and relaxed
- *Using prayer:* people with a faith will have access to particular spiritual routes into a meditative state – for example, you can draw on prayer to help stimulate reflection on a chosen topic.

There are also structured mindfulness exercises, which include the body scan and walking meditation.

### Find Out More

Granger, T. (2019). *Draw Breath: The Art of Breathing, Mindfulness and Meditation.* London: Hachette.

Greenhaigh, W. A. (2015). *Mindfulness and the Art of Drawing: A Creative Path to Awareness.* Lewis, East Sussex: Leaping Hare Press.

## Visualisation

Visualisation is a mental training technique often used by elite athletes. By imagining a successful future event, they can play out how an event might occur in their minds. This is a powerful technique because it allows you to rehearse what success would look like. In our context, reflective practitioners can visualise themselves achieving their positive intention.

### You Will Need

- Some protected time (a minimum of ten minutes).
- A quiet space for reflection.

### How to Use Visualisation

First, allocate some time to the exercise. It is helpful to minimise the risk of interruption or distraction. If you can find a quiet, relaxing space for this activity, that is ideal.

Second, take a moment to relax, perhaps by taking three deep breaths. This will be time for you to enjoy imagining your own future success.

Third, use your imagination to think about how it would feel to achieve your positive intention. What emotions would you be experiencing? What would you see around you? What are the sounds, sights and smell of success? Try to add as much detail and vividness as you can to what you are imagining.

Fourth, reflect on what others around you would notice when you are achieving your positive intention. What are they saying, doing or thinking? Thinking about your potential personal and professional impact can be very motivating.

Finally, capture in writing or drawing some of the most important insights that emerged during this exercise.

## Mindmapping

Developed by Tony Buzan (2018), mindmaps are a visual tool for organising and setting out your ideas. Their strengths are in their immediate applicability and simplicity. Mindmapping encourages the free flow of thoughts and makes it possible to see connections and opportunities that may not otherwise have come to mind. The process can also remind you of ideas or concepts that you may have forgotten to include in your thinking. Most importantly, for the purposes of reflective practice, this tool can be used to explore very complex topics.

The process is designed to counterbalance a tendency to think in a linear, logical way by encouraging you to 'think aloud' and free your mind to make connections as you draw. Mindmapping is especially useful when you would like to see how ideas connect with one another. It is also helpful when a 'big picture' view is needed.

### You Will Need

- A blank sheet of paper.
- Some pencils or pens of differing colours.

## How to Mindmap

1. Set out your central idea or topic somewhere near the centre of the page. This will be the focus of your exploration. Throughout this process, be succinct in your explanation of the ideas – ideally using a word or a short phrase to capture each concept.
2. Draw some lines radiating outwards from the central theme. These are like branches that grow out from a tree. Each one of these will be a key new concept or idea that emerges from the central theme. Add as many branches as necessary, labelling each with a word or short phrase.
3. The newly created concepts or ideas now become the central themes for the next level of sub-branches. Now you will have branches emanating out of the new ideas that you had identified earlier. All of this work emerges from the central theme and you can grow the mindmap as much as necessary.
4. Now that you have quite a few ideas drawn out in front of you, look for possible connections or associations. How are the ideas linked? What is missing? What might need to be highlighted? Use different coloured pencils or pens to show how certain ideas relate to others, or to add missing concepts, or to highlight important realisations.
5. Refine your mindmap to include any new insights that may have emerged. You can use different colours to show how some of the concepts may be related to others. Similarly, you can use colours to indicate level of importance or priority.
6. Capture your learning from this creative activity, being especially alert to new connections or insights that you have gained.

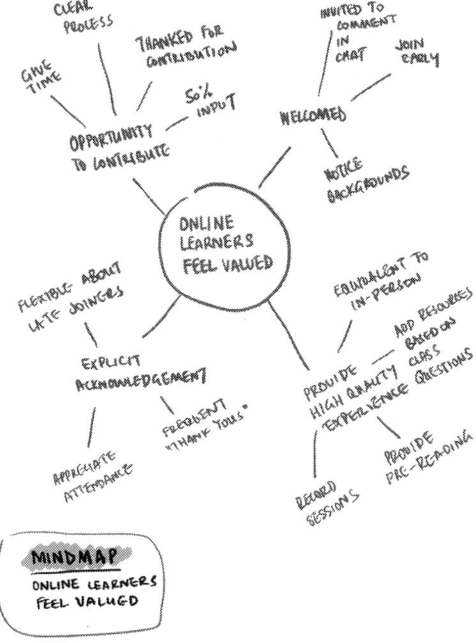


**Figure A3.7** Mindmapping

### Alternative Approach

There are apps to support mindmapping (e.g. MindMeister, XMind and Mind Mapping), and this process can also be completed on a tablet, laptop or personal computer. The choice of which to use is down to your personal preference.

**Find Out More**

Buzan, T. (2018). *Mindmap Mastery*. London: Watkins Publishing.

## Ask a Chatbot

In this activity, we will be interacting with a chatbot to generate creative ideas. Chatbots are excellent sources of information and data. Because your chatbot's responses are generated by artificial intelligence, you will be responding to existing ideas or addressing contemporary questions to generate creative ideas that are specific to you.

### You Will Need

- A laptop, device or mobile telephone.
- Access to a chatbot.

### How to Ask a Chatbot

1 Select the topic for exploration. This should be related to your reflective practice.
2 Ask the chatbot: 'what is the best way to think about [your topic]?' Take some time to read and reflect on the response.
3 Ask the chatbot to provide you with four ways of addressing your topic. Once the answers are generated, look through to see what resonates the most. What new ideas have emerged for you?
4 Capture these insights and use them as part of your reflective practice process.

### Alternatively

You can put an idea into the chatbot and ask it for its opinion. When it provides an opinion, you can follow up with 'what other ways are there for thinking about this?'

## Elevator Pitch

The so-called 'elevator pitch' is a concise summary of a product or service. It takes its name from the idea that the pitch can be presented in the time it takes to ride an elevator. A good elevator pitch should be engaging whilst providing the key points of an idea or product. Use your phone or device to video record an elevator pitch about what you are hoping to achieve through your reflective practice.

### You Will Need

- A video recording device.
- A quiet space for recording.

### How to Prepare your Elevator Pitch

1. Prepare a script that includes all the main points that you would like to convey in a 30–90 second video. Make sure you are clear about the purpose of your reflective practice – and also how you are going to achieve your desired outcome.
2. Practise delivering your script out loud. Make any refinements or edits to ensure it is as clear, concise and engaging as possible.
3. Using your mobile phone or other video recording device, record yourself delivering the elevator pitch. It is best to record the video in a quiet location.
4. Watch the video. What becomes clearer to you as you watch the video? What creative ideas emerge about how to proceed?

### Alternatively

Once the video is ready, share it with friends or close colleagues. Ask for their feedback. What would make the elevator pitch more engaging or clear?

## METHODS REQUIRING UP TO 30 MINUTES

### Using Visual Images

Pictures provide a stimulating way to enable you to see things from different angles. They can be particularly helpful when you are stuck and cannot see a way past obstacles. Visual images, as advertisers know, have a powerful emotional impact on people. Introducing pictures into your reflective practice can be a very effective way of encouraging important feelings to be surfaced and their impacts to be explored.

### You Will Need

- A set of coloured photographs – say ten in total, showing a variety of situations. The greater the diversity and the more abstract, the better. You can use your own photographs or curate your own collection from the various free access image websites on the internet. Or you could just cut them out of magazines. Alternatively, you can purchase a set specifically designed for use in development activities (as illustrated in the example provided in the box below).

## Abstract Images

### How to Use this Method

1 There are many ways to use pictures in reflective practice. No doubt you will be able to come up with your own variations. One way is to use them to establish the present state and desired future for your reflective intention. Begin by laying out your set of pictures so you can see them all.
2 Select a picture that speaks to you in some way about the current position of your reflective intention. It is a good idea to make your choice very quickly just going with the image that stands out from the rest. In this way you can minimise the possibilities of the logical part of your brain kicking in to influence your choice.
3 Reflect on what connections you can make between your intention and the image. What emotions are you experiencing as you view the image? Spend some time exploring the possibilities here and brainstorming the implications. What assumptions might you be making that need to be confirmed or challenged?
4 The process is repeated with a picture selected for its connections to a desired future state.
5 With the present and future states fully explored you can turn to working on how to move progressively towards the desired outcome.
6 You might want to keep a record of your explorations. Taking a photograph of your chosen pictures can be a helpful reminder when you look back later.

Alternatively: You can do this activity virtually, on your phone, tablet or laptop computer. Follow the instructions above, using your 'photos' app to create a folder for the images you would like to use.

A version of this text was first published in Passmore, J., Day, C., Flower, J., Grieve, M. & Moon, J. J. (Eds.) (2023). *Coaching Tools: A Further 123 Coaching Tools and Techniques for Executive Coaches, Team Coaches, Mentors and Supervisors: Volume 2*. Farringdon, Oxon: Libri Publishing.

## Reflecting on Relationships

This method, extracted and adapted from Hawkins and Smith (2013), is very useful for reflecting on the quality of relationships between people and the emotional factors that are in play. Again, there are many ways to approach examining a relationship (for example, between a professional and their client).

- Removing the relationship from the professional setting and placing it in a different context – how does the relationship fare now that you have met on a hike up Mount Kilimanjaro?
- Thinking back to your last meeting with the client. You are a fly on the wall observing the interaction – what becomes immediately obvious about the nature of the relationship and your interactions together?

- Considering what would happen if the two of you were marooned together on a desert island with little hope of rescue or contact with others – what would happen and what does this tell you about the relationship?

You can draw on your responses to scenarios such as these to gain insights into the relationship you have with the client, which can then form the foundation for reflecting on how things might need to change by accentuating the strengths and addressing any weaknesses.

### Find Out More

Hawkins, P. & Smith, N. (2013). *Coaching, Mentoring and Organizational Consultancy: Supervision, Skills and Development*. 2nd edn. Maidenhead: Open University Press.

## Sketching

Sketching has all the benefits discussed previously in relation to visual imagery. In addition, as you will be involved in creating the image it will capture the factors that are most important to you.

Sketching taps into ways of seeing that talking alone does not always reach, including the emotional content embodied in the topic being explored. Sketching can seem tentative and easier to change. Colours and abstract shapes can become powerful representations of your feelings about a subject that might otherwise be difficult to talk about, or to find the words to express. Engaging visually really helps when you are 'stuck for words'. Your sketch might be a representation … or it could be an abstract image comprised of, for example, colours, shapes and patterns. Another option is to construct a collaged image.

When the sketch is a cartoon, the inclusion of humour adds another dimension (see later in this appendix). This can produce insights through the juxtaposition of different, unrelated ideas or the exposure of absurdities. This is an excellent way of bringing your playful side to your reflective practice.

### You Will Need

- Felt-tipped pens, pencils and/or crayons in a variety of colours.
- Sheets of plain paper (A4 or A3).

### How to Use this Method

1 Create a sketch that depicts the core features of your reflective intention. A starting point for a sketch might be a metaphor (e.g. 'It's like wading through treacle …'). The artistic merit of what you produce is irrelevant as the sketch only needs to make sense to you.
2 Once you have completed your sketch, take a good, hard look at what you have created. Start with what the whole image means to you and what it says about the topic you are exploring.

3 Then focus in on each of the details of your image such as colours, shapes and thickness of lines. What significance might they have? Keep the focus on your intention for the reflective practice. Often the *process* of producing the sketch is revelatory in some way – for instance, in giving validation to some strong feelings or in developing a greater understanding of the driving forces in a situation. What did you put more energy into producing? When and why did you pause? Which parts of your image did you put the most energy into?

A version of this text was first published in Passmore, J., Day, C., Flower, J., Grieve, M. & Moon, J. J. (Eds.) (2022). *Coaching Tools: A Further 123 Coaching Tools and Techniques for Executive Coaches, Team Coaches, Mentors and Supervisors: Volume 2*. Farringdon, Oxon: Libri Publishing.

### Find Out More

Edwards, B. (2003). *The New Drawing on the Right Side of the Brain Workbook*. London: Souvenir Press.

Edwards, B. (2008). *The New Drawing on the Right Side of the Brain*. London: Harper Collins.

The School of Life. (2021). *Drawing as Therapy*. London: The School of Life.

Sheather, A. (2019). *Coaching Beyond Words: Using Art to Deepen and Enrich Our Conversations*. Abingdon: Routledge. Visit Anna at artincoaching.co.uk for blogs and resources.

Watts, A. (2022). *Collage as a Creative Coaching Tool: A Comprehensive Resource for Coaches and Psychologists*. Abingdon: Routledge. Visit Andrea at unglueyou.co.uk for collaging resources.

## Reading Poetry

Poetry can enable us to access emotions and ways of seeing that are fresh and insightful. It can stimulate our creativity and generate empathy with others. Poems can be used in a number of ways in reflective practice.

### How to Use this Method

1 Choose a favourite or random poem from an anthology.
2 Spend time finding connections between the ideas and sentiments and the topic you wish to explore.
3 Analyse the poem and notice how the poet expresses emotions and ideas. What insights does this give you about your positive intention?

### Find Out More

Foster, T. C. (2018). *How to Read Poetry Like a Professor*. New York: Harper Perennial.

## Writing Poetry

You can write your own poem related to your positive intention. You might start from a phrase or set of words that has some relevance in the situation you are exploring, making this the first line of your poem. You can also adopt different styles such as a limerick or a haiku. Or you can create a poem that has no particular structure. Remember, a poem does not always have to rhyme or have a particular rhythm or shape. You are writing the poem for your own purposes.

### How to Use this Method

1 Write down your poem.
2 Having completed your poem, consider how the overall sentiment and the component parts connect with the focus of your reflective endeavour.

**Table A3.2** Haiku examples

| **An example of 'before and after' haikus** | |
|---|---|
| Before | After |
| After the day's strife | I am not alone |
| I burn the candle both ends | Making space to talk things out |
| Forever alone | Links me to the world |

### Find Out More

Holder, J. (2013). *49 Ways to Write Yourself Well*. Brighton: Step Beach Press.
Klanchy, K. (2023). *How to Grow Your Own Poem*. London: Swift Press.

## Modelling

### You Will Need

A selection of objects (totalling six to eight) you can use to create a model or a sculpture. You can use any small objects that are to hand.

**Figure A3.8** Modelling

This is a tactile approach that will appeal to practitioners with a kinaesthetic learning preference and involves constructing a model or 'sculpture' about the topic you wish to explore in your reflective practice. Each element in the model represents an aspect of that topic. Like the constellations approach (see later in this appendix), this technique lends itself to the exploration of relationships between people or ideas and the system in which those relationships are embedded. It is based on the Lego Serious Play approach for expressing thoughts, reflections and ideas. For more about this and other ways to incorporate play into your reflective practice see Stephanie Wheeler and Teresa Leyman's book: *Playfulness in Coaching: Exploring Our Untapped Potential through Playfulness, Creativity and Imagination*.

## How to Use this Method

1. Create a model by placing the objects in relation to one another that speaks in some way to you about the topic you want to explore. Be intuitive rather than logical or rational. This approach works best when you get your hands to 'do the thinking', rather than your head.
2. Allow yourself a maximum of five minutes for the model to be created. An immediate, speedy response is important to minimise over-thinking. It is also best to not attribute any particular qualities to each of the objects – they shouldn't be literal representations of people or entities.

3 Ask yourself: What emotions are embedded in the model, either in the construction as a whole or in the individual component parts?
4 Explore the systemic factors that might be affecting the situation being explored.
5 As you review your model, focus in on any possible implications of:

- colour, shape, size, height, width, texture
- any links between different objects or the lack of links between them
- closeness or distance between the different parts of the model
- the overall organisation of the model – is it a tidy or messy construction?

6 Explore the meaning of the whole model as a single entity, and of each of the constituent parts – what purpose do they have in the scheme of things?
7 Stand up, move around and view your model from different angles – what insights are gained from the various viewpoints?
8 It can be useful to keep a record of your initial construction – so take a photograph of the model.
9 Having explored this first construction of your model, you can now adjust the components to create a new configuration that depicts, in some way, a changed situation. Notice how you touch and move the objects. For example, which ones do you choose to move first, and why? What significance might these tactile data have?
10 Again, you may wish to photograph the revised model so you have a record for future use.
11 You could repeat this process to establish a number of stages towards a conclusion.
12 Focus on the emotions depicted in the model and those generated by its creation.
13 Focus on the positive elements in play. How might you deploy these to meet the positive intention you are exploring?
14 Similarly, focus on the obstacles and distractions that are impeding progress towards a better situation; remember that some barriers may actually be helpful. For example, delaying a decision (rather than procrastination) might be an appropriate response in some circumstances.
15 Having explored your revised model or models, what might you keep doing, stop doing, do more of and less of? What are you willing to change, or give up?
16 Finally, capture the insights and learning you have gained from exploring the model(s).

## Alternative Approach

Like the constellations approach, you can use this process to model relationships between people or ideas in a system. In this alternative approach, you begin by assigning the objects to the people or functions that make up the system and use the process described above to explore the relationships involved in the generation of the outcomes the system is designed to achieve.

**Figure A3.9** Modelling completed

*Model and photos by David – part of a personal exploration into increasing the role of art creation in his life.*

## Find Out More

Kristiansen, P. & Rasmussen, R. (2014). *Building a Better Business Using the Lego Serious Play Method.* Hoboken, NJ: Wiley.

Wheeler, S. & Leyman, T. (2024). *Playfulness in Coaching: Exploring Our Untapped Potential through Playfulness, Creativity and Imagination.* Abingdon: Routledge.

## Mindfulness – Walking Meditation

Many people find walking, particularly in open spaces, conducive to reflection. Find somewhere pleasant to walk and follow the process below.

### How to Use this Method

1 Before going out, clarify your positive intention, then set it aside to let it percolate as you walk.

2 Make deliberate efforts to pay attention to the detail of your surroundings (for example, the sights and sounds, the flora and fauna).

3 Pay attention also to noticing the sensations in your body as you walk and your breathing.

4 Towards the end of your walk, as you return to your base, allow your reflective intention to come back into view – what images, emotions or thoughts arise for you? Capture these in whatever way feels appropriate.

In addition to insights and learning, creativity can be used to record, for example, the outcomes of your experiments. Rather than capturing your data in note form, you might want to capture your thoughts, ideas and feelings as mindmaps, doodles, collages, sketches, poems, songs or video recordings.

## Mindfulness - Body Scan

The body scan is a quick and straightforward way of feeling more grounded. It can be undertaken in any quiet, relaxing space.

### How to Use this Method

1. Before starting, clarify your positive intention.
2. Sit comfortably on a chair with your feet placed firmly on the floor, your arms supported on your thighs and your eyes closed.
3. Focus your attention on each part of your body in turn – in each case noticing and removing any tension.
4. Starting with your feet – feel them supported by the floor and imagine them connected through the floor and out of the building to the earth beneath.
5. Move your attention to your shins and calves, then your thighs and back supported by the chair, then your lower abdomen and chest and finally, your neck and head.
6. Imagine a thread connecting your head to the ceiling, holding it erect; imagine the thread passing through the ceiling and the roof of your building and connecting you to the sky and the universe above.
7. Throughout the body scan pay attention to your breathing – breathe in for six counts, and breathe out for eight counts, the out-breath always slightly longer than the in-breath.
8. Throughout the scan notice any sounds around you – acknowledge their existence and set them aside; similarly, notice any thoughts that come into your mind, acknowledge that they are there and set them aside.
9. When you are ready, become aware again of your surroundings, slowly open your eyes and come back into your space.
10. As you emerge from the meditation, what images, emotions or thoughts about your reflective intention occur to you? Capture these in whatever way feels appropriate.

## Email from Someone Important

Spoiler alert: *You* are the important person. Designed to encourage perspective-taking, this activity invites you to draft an email that a future version of you might send to the current version of you. It may sound eccentric, but it is a great way to give yourself some distance from a situation that may be front of mind at a given time.

### You Will Need

- An email account.
- A computer, tablet or mobile phone.

### How to Do this Activity

1. Think of a time in the future that is relatively distant (normally one to five years). Imagine that you have been successful in achieving your positive intention.
2. Imagine that you are now in the future, as a successful professional. From this future perspective, draft an email to the current version of yourself. Start with a normal salutation (to yourself), and then draft one or two paragraphs of advice or guidance from your new position in the future.
3. Make sure that you are encouraging and compassionate in your message. It is meant to empower and motivate you.
4. Save the message as a draft. Take a short break and come back to the email. What insights emerge? What is important for you to consider? What has the different perspective allowed you to understand better?

### Alternatively

You may prefer to hand-write the letter to yourself. In this case, treat it like a letter with appropriate greetings at the start and end. Finally, put it in an envelope so that you can revisit the letter at a later time.

## Listen to Yourself Better

We all have self-talk – but how often do we take time to listen to what it is saying? In this activity, bring that talk into the open by audio recording a message to yourself. What would you like to say to yourself as you work towards your positive intention? This is a creative way to adapt your self-talk to support you as you engage in reflective practice.

### You Will Need

- An audio recording device.

### How to Listen to Yourself Better

1 Bring to your awareness any 'self-talk' that you engage in as you work towards your positive intention. What sort of things do you say to yourself?
2 Audio record a few of the things that you say to yourself. For example, 'I'm not good at presenting my ideas clearly'.
3 Listen to the recording. How helpful is this self-talk to you? If it is helpful, keep using it. If not, think of more positive things that you can say to yourself as you work towards your positive intention. In relation to the previous example, you might switch it to 'I'm getting better at presenting my ideas clearly and with confidence' or 'I enjoy sharing ideas that make a difference to people'.
4 Now record the new phrase or sentence that you have selected. How does it feel when you listen to that? If it is encouraging and helpful, adopt the new phrase.

### Alternatively

Audio record daily brief reflections about progress you are making towards your desired future outcome. Review these reflections every week as a way of acknowledging your progress and paying attention to your thoughts and emotions as you work towards your professional goals.

# METHODS REQUIRING 60+ MINUTES

## Story-Telling

Stories are evocative and provide valuable ways of shifting your perspective on a topic. Moving the action to a fictional third party and imagining how they might respond when faced with your real-life topic frees you from the everyday constraints that can block your thinking.

Joseph Campbell's notion of the hero's journey (2014) describes the core elements of powerful storytelling which underpin films like *Lord of the Rings* and *Star Wars*. No doubt you will recognise the narrative arc of the journey in these movies. Using this process, you will be able to use storytelling to construct a narrative focused on your own role as the protagonist. This works particularly well when your positive intention involves facing a challenge, especially a daunting one.

### How to Use this Method

1 *The call to adventure:* Focusing on the challenge you face, explore the details of what is drawing you to take action. This might include thinking about your personal values, the external pressures that are driving change and a consideration of why you might be reluctant to engage with the challenge (e.g. lack of skill, experience or motivation).
2 *Crossing a threshold:* This step marks the beginning of the major transformation, which is central to your story and involves the protagonist

moving into unknown territory. Explore what stepping into the unknown looks and feels like. What personal resources can you call on?

3 *Acquiring a mentor:* In the archetypal story, the protagonist meets someone with the powers and resources that can make an impact on the challenge through positive guidance – someone who can perhaps offer a 'magical power'. Identify and incorporate this person as a character into your story and think about what resources they might provide for your journey.
4 *Finding helpers:* The protagonist meets and assembles a group of like-minded individuals who join their quest. These individuals may also feel daunted by the task at hand, but they are determined. Identify people who might provide you with camaraderie to help you with the task and incorporate them as characters into your story, identifying the qualities and resources they bring.
5 *The revelation:* As the protagonist in this story, describe the struggles on the journey towards your goal. Now you arrive at a critical point in the journey where your very survival is threatened, but you manage to find the personal resources to prevail. In the story, your survival may be related to some magical power or intervention. What is the worst-case scenario that could happen? Start to discover the personal (and other) resources available to you for addressing the challenge.
6 *The return home:* As the protagonist, you return home with your comrades and share anecdotes about the group's adventures with those who stayed behind. In the retelling of your story, celebrate your successes and share the insights gained from the adventure.

### Find Out More

Campbell, J. (2014). *The Hero's Journey: Joseph Campbell on His Life and Work.* Toronto: New World.

Fulford, R. (1999). *The Triumph of the Narrative: Storytelling in the Age of Mass Culture.* New York: Broadway.

## Constellations

The constellations method (Whittington, 2020) is a way of depicting a set of relationships within a system – between individuals, groups of people, functions or organisations. It can also be used to map the connections between ideas. The approach is particularly useful in enabling you to understand your relationships with others, including in a team, between teams or within partnerships of organisations.

Constellations are visual representations of a system using objects and they therefore also have a tactile element to them. The tactile properties of the objects add another dimension, which can help stimulate your insights and learning, particularly if you have a kinaesthetic (tactile) learning preference.

## You Will Need

- A set of plastic pawns or counters, or a random set of small objects (like buttons, shells, or pebbles).
- A board or tabletop to arrange your objects.

## How to Use this Method

1. *Choose the focus:* Once you have identified your focus, the physical boundary of the constellation needs to be decided. You will need some way of marking out where the system that you are thinking about begins and ends. This might simply be the edges of the board or tabletop you are working on. Otherwise, you could use masking tape to designate an area on the floor.
2. *Create the constellation:* Start to create a map of the relationships that have significance for your positive intention. At this stage, the focus is on the current quality of the relationships, rather than how they might be changed. Begin by choosing an object to represent you and place it in an appropriate position on the board or tabletop. Each object placed in the constellation represents a key player in the system. With each addition, think about *why* that person is important in the system. The positioning of the objects and the distance between each is a vital way of representing the strengths of the relationships between the key people – the closer the objects, the stronger the relationship. When you have finished mapping the current state of your significant relationships, check to make sure you have included everyone of importance and represented the strength of your relationship with each of them accurately.
3. *Notice and analyse:* Now your constellation is complete, view what has been constructed. What are your immediate impressions, thoughts and feelings? Explore your constellation and the relationships in detail to gain a deeper and broader understanding of the current situation. It can be helpful for you to take up different positions in the constellation in order to view the system from different perspectives. How effective is this system? What evidence do you have for your assertions? Give some thought to features such as:

    - how long the different players have been involved – this can influence a sense of belonging in the system
    - how people feel about their involvement and each other, including the value people perceive they have in relation to others
    - how individual values affect relationships
    - the degrees of collaboration and competition
    - the informal connections between people and how these impact the formal relationships
    - the balance of giving and receiving between people (e.g. of resources, of motivational support)
    - how aligned people are with the outcomes the system exists to achieve.

It can be a good idea to take a photograph of your constellation so you have a record of the current reality for reference later in this process.

1 *Make movements:* Having analysed the current state of the system you can now move people around the constellation, noticing what difference each specific movement makes in relation to your original positive intention. Make these movements slowly to allow space for reflection about their impact. To what extent does a specific movement tend to improve or worsen the strength of relationships and the effectiveness of the system?
2 *Dismantle the constellation:* As you slowly take your constellation apart and put away the objects, give some thought to the insights and learning you have generated and their implications for your thinking and behaviour as part of the system. What will you need to do to move closer to your positive intention?

### Find Out More

Whittington, J. (2020). *Systemic Coaching and Constellations: The Principles, Practices and Application for Groups, Teams and Individuals.* 3rd edn. London: Kogan Page.

## Storyboarding

While mindmapping is intentionally designed to encourage non-linear thinking, storyboarding does the opposite. Used by filmmakers, animators and marketing professionals, this technique will allow you to develop a narrative by creating a sequence of images that tell a story. Storyboarding is especially helpful when planning ahead.

### You Will Need

- A blank sheet of paper.
- Pens or pencils.

### How to Storyboard

1 It is necessary for you to decide the length of the 'story' that you would like to explore. This means deciding the beginning and end of the story. When using this in the context of reflective practice, the end point will usually be when you have achieved your desired outcome.
2 Identify the main elements, characters and setting of the story. You will need to decide on these as you start to work on your storyboard.
3 Draw a series of frames (squares or rectangles, see example). For the purposes of reflective practice, we would recommend between four and eight frames.
4 Sketch or draw a scene in the first and final frames. These should represent the present time (first frame) and the desired future outcome (last frame). When sketching, decide whether some annotation or dialogue (using speech bubbles) may be helpful.

5 Do some reflection and plan out the intervening scenes. Once the order is clear in your mind, sketch in the remaining frames. Again, decide whether some annotation or dialogue (using speech bubbles) may be helpful.
6 Now that you have the completed storyboard, look over it to see what new insights have emerged. What is the central theme? What needs to happen between now and the final frame? What or who is missing? What else needs to be added?

**Figure A3.10** Storyboarding

## Alternative Approach

You may prefer to get an external perspective on the storyboard. In this case, when you have completed the storyboard ask a friend or colleague to look at the storyboard and share their impressions. How do they see this story unfolding?

A version of this text was first published in Passmore, J., Day, C., Flower, J., Grieve, M. & Moon, J. J. (Eds.). (2023). *Coaching Tools: A Further 123 Coaching Tools and Techniques for Executive Coaches, Team Coaches, Mentors and Supervisors: Volume 2*. Farringdon, Oxon: Libri Publishing.

### Find Out More

Sibbet, D. (2010). *Visual Meetings: How Graphics, Sticky Notes and Idea Mapping Can Transform Group Productivity*. Mahwah, NJ: Wiley.

## Cartooning

Some cartoons make you laugh out loud. Some cartoons don't – but they point out absurdities, causing a wry smile of recognition in the process. Cartoonists, particularly political cartoonists, draw on five key elements to create impact:

1 *Analogy* – a comparison between two unlike things that share some characteristics
2 *Symbolism* – using an object to represent an idea
3 *Irony* – the difference between the way things are and the way things should be or are expected to be
4 *Exaggeration* – overstating or magnifying a problem, physical feature or habit
5 *Labelling and captioning* – to clarify an idea.

**Figure A3.11** Creating impact through cartooning

You can use these ideas to get down to the fundamentals of a reflective intention you wish to explore. Cartooning is a powerful means of storytelling – it is not just a form of sketching, it is a way of *seeing*, which can offer a new window into a situation.

Cartoons offer opportunities to:

- create caricatures
- illustrate the pantomime nature of some aspects of organisational life
- invoke satire as a way of understanding challenging situations
- exaggerate and subvert stereotypes
- make connections to important systemic factors
- unearth influential aspects of organisational culture – or life more generally.

Simple elements can combine in complex ways and this can be a powerful source of insight. More broadly, we know that humour has positive health and wellbeing impacts.

Cartooning can help when you are stuck and a radically different lens is helpful. You may have already found some humour in the situation you are reflecting upon. Cartooning will amplify that comedic element. You can also use cartooning to explore a metaphor that has relevance to your reflections.

## You Will Need

- Sheets of paper (at least A4 size and enough for several attempts, where necessary) and a variety of coloured pens and markers, including black; bold black outlines make for stronger images.
- A tablet with note-taking or drawing app.

## How to Use Cartooning

1 Firstly, be assured that there is no imperative to create the quality of image that you will see on a daily basis in newspapers or magazines. You are using this approach for your own purposes and the only person who needs to understand what it represents is you. Set aside any concerns you might have about a 'childish comic-like' approach. In this arena, remember that anything goes. Be playful!

2 Like everyone, you can create cartoons using basic shapes (e.g. circles, ovals, squares, rectangles, triangles and diamonds). You can doodle stick figures and use dots and lines to make simple but expressive faces. You can add speech and thought bubbles to add further observations and humour. Brief captions can help to explain or highlight what is going on in the image – however, it is a good idea to try to keep the words to a minimum.

**Figure A3.12** Expressive faces

1. Identify a favourite cartoonist. What do you like about that person's approach? What particular characteristics of their cartoons are you drawn to?
2. In sketching out your cartoon, replicate some of the approaches cartoonists take (particularly political cartoonists because they focus on issues):
   - juxtapose contradictory ideas
   - find humour in everything – even the darkest topics
   - point up the absurdities of a situation or life in general
   - notice patterns and discrepancies
   - cut straight to the essence of a topic
   - mine metaphors for their significance
   - create caricatures and satire
   - sketch in unrealistic or semi-realistic ways.
3. As you create a cartoon focused on your positive intention, try to avoid analysing what is emerging – that will come later in this process.
4. When you have a completed cartoon, take a good look at the different elements of the cartoon. Who is depicted? What are they doing? What is funny or even absurd? Who, or what might be missing? How have you deployed humour, symbolism, exaggeration, irony, analogy, labelling, caricature or satire?
5. What significance do these observations have for your positive intention? What are the wider impacts on relationships with others? What might be the systemic implications? What insights and learning can you draw out of these

deliberations? What will you do now with this learning? How will it change your thinking, behaviour and professional practice?

6 What have you discovered that illuminates your positive intention?

Versions of this text were first published in:

Passmore, J., Day, C., Flower, J., Grieve, M. & Moon, J. J. (2023). *Coaching Tools: A Further 123 Coaching Tools and Techniques for Executive Coaches, Team Coaches, Mentors and Supervisors: Volume 3*. Farringdon, Oxon: Libri Publishing.

Love, D. (2023). You've got to laugh: Cartooning in coaching and supervision. Association for Coaching's *Coaching Perspectives* magazine, April 2023, Issue 37, p. 42.

**Find Out More**

Chapman, R. (2012). *Drawing Comics: 52 Exercises on Characters, Panels, Storytelling, Publishing and Professional Practices*. Beverley, MA: Quarry Books.

## FINAL REFLECTION

These are a selected sample of the myriad ways in which you are able to incorporate creativity into your reflective practice. We hope that you are willing to experiment with some of these techniques. You may continue using your own creative practices or identify other strategies that will bring energy and new ideas into your work. Of course, the internet is another rich source of numerous, diverse approaches to creativity.

While the techniques presented here will certainly bring creativity into your process of Effective Reflective Practice, they have other benefits too. First, they will keep the process of reflective practice fresh, engaging and alive. Second, they are likely to enhance your wellbeing too. The more energised, engaged and well you are, the better it is for your clients and your work.

# APPENDIX 4
## UNDERTAKING AN EQUALITY IMPACT ASSESSMENT ON YOUR PLAN

The purpose of an Equality Impact Assessment (EIA) is to gauge the actual or potential implications of your planned actions for different people. This will include the impact on existing clients, other stakeholders and colleagues. Your EIA should also consider other people who you might reasonably expect to become clients or stakeholders in the future. For instance, you may work in an area with a diverse population, some sections of which may not currently be involved with the service you provide. In this case you will also want to take in how your plan might include reaching out to those groups. Essentially, you are looking to avoid the unintended consequences of negative impacts *and* to plan in actions that will promote and achieve equality and inclusion.

Your EIA should focus on age, caring responsibilities, disability (including mental health disabilities), gender reassignment, marriage and civil partnership, neurodiversity, pregnancy and maternity, race, religion, sexual orientation and socio-economic factors. There may also be other groups of clients and stakeholders who have a particular involvement with the service you provide.

Questions to think about include:

- What are the actual or potential impacts of your planned actions?
- What will you do to mitigate the negative and enhance the positive impacts?
- How do you propose to manage any emerging unintended consequences?
- What language is appropriate to use with individual clients? For example, what terminology do they each prefer to use to describe themselves?
- What are the intersectionality implications of your plan, i.e. how do different social factors combine to shape people's experience of your service?

# REFERENCES


Argyris, C. (1993). *Knowledge for Action: A Guide to Overcoming Barriers to Organizational Change*. San Francisco, CA: Jossey Bass.

Arnott, A. (2013). *Positive Failure: Understand How Embracing Failure is a Tool for Development*. Liverpool: Liverpool Academic Press.

Boyatzis, R. (2006). An overview of intentional change from a complexity perspective. *Journal of Management Development 25*(7): 607–23.

Brown, S. (2010). *Play: How it Shapes the Brain, Opens the Imagination and Invigorates the Soul*. London: Penguin.

Bruner, J. S. (1960). The Process of Education. Cambridge, MA: Harvard University Press.

Buzan, T. (2018). *Mindmap Mastery*. London: Watkins Publishing.

Campbell, J. (2014). *The Hero's Journey: Joseph Campbell on His Life and Work*. Toronto: New World.

Csikszentmihalyi, M. (1990). *Flow: The Psychology of Optimal Performance*. New York: Harper and Row.

Csikszentmihalyi, M. (2013). *Creativity: The Psychology of Discovery and Invention*. New York: Harper Perennial.

Deloitte (2020). *Deloitte Insights: The Social Enterprise at Work – Paradox as a Path Forward*. Deloitte Global Human Capital Trends.

Dewey, J. (1910). *How we Think: A Restatement of the Relation of Reflective Thinking to the Educative Process*. Boston: Heath & Co.

Edwards, B. (2003). *The New Drawing on the Right Side of the Brain Workbook*. London: Souvenir Press.

Edwards, B. (2008). *The New Drawing on the Right Side of the Brain*. London: Harper Collins.

Edwards, S. (2017). Reflecting differently. New dimensions: reflection-before-action and reflection-beyond-action. *International Practice Development Journal* 7: 1–14.

Elliot, A. J. & Friedman, R. (2007). Approach-avoidance: A central characteristic of personal goals. In B. R. Little, K. Salmela-Aro & S. D. Phillips (Eds.), *Personal Project Pursuit: Goals, Actions, and Human Flourishing* (pp. 97–118). Mahwah, NJ: Lawrence Erlbaum.

Foster, T. C. (2018). *How to Read Poetry Like a Professor*. New York: Harper Perennial.

Fulford, R. (1999). *The Triumph of the Narrative: Storytelling in the Age of Mass Culture*. New York: Broadway.

Gibbs, G. (1988). *Learning by Doing: A Guide to Teaching and Learning Methods*. Further Education Unit. Oxford: Oxford Polytechnic.

Granger, T. (2019). *Draw Breath: The Art of Breathing, Mindfulness and Meditation*. London: Hachette.

Greenhaigh, W. A. (2015). *Mindfulness and the Art of Drawing: A Creative Path to Awareness*. Lewis, East Sussex: Leaping Hare Press.

Gregory, D. (2006). *The Creative License: Giving Yourself Permission to Be the Artist You Truly Are*. New York: Hachette.

Hawkins, P. & Smith, N. (2013). *Coaching, Mentoring and Organizational Consultancy: Supervision, Skills and Development*. 2nd edn. Maidenhead: Open University Press.

Holder, J. (2013). *49 Ways to Write Yourself Well*. Brighton: Step Beach Press.

Honey, P. & Mumford, A. (1982). *The Manual of Learning Styles*. Maidenhead: Peter Honey.

Honey, P. & Mumford, A. (1986). *Learning Styles Questionnaire*. London: Peter Honey Publications.

Honey, P. & Mumford, A. (2006). *The Learning Styles Questionnaire, 80-item version*. Maidenhead: Peter Honey.

Jarden, A. & Jarden, R. (2022). Learn about yourself. In C. van Nieuwerburgh & P. Williams (Eds.), *From Surviving to Thriving: A Student's Guide to Feeling and Doing Well at University* (pp. 127–38). London: Sage.

James, A. (2020). Reflective practice in coaching. In J. Passmore (Ed.), *The Complete Practitioner Guide for Professional Coaches*. Abingdon: Routledge.

Kemmis, S. (1985). Action research and the politics of reflection. In D. Boud, R. Keogh and D. Walker (Eds.), *Reflection: Turning Experience into Learning*. New York: Kogan Page.

Klanchy, K. (2023). *How to Grow Your Own Poem*. London: Swift Press.

Kline, N. (2002). *Time to Think. Listening to Ignite the Human Mind*. London: Cassell.

Kolb, D. A. (1984). *Experiential Learning: Experience as the Source of Learning and Development*. Englewood Cliffs, NJ: Prentice-Hall.

Kristiansen, P. & Rasmussen, R. (2014). *Building a Better Business Using the Lego Serious Play Method*. Hoboken, NJ: Wiley.

Levitin, D (2019). *This Is Your Brain on Music: Understanding a Human Obsession*. London: Penguin.

Locke, E. A. & Latham, G. P. (2002). Building a practically useful theory of goal setting and task motivation. *American Psychologist 57*(9): 705–17.

Love, D. (2023). You've got to laugh: Cartooning in coaching and supervision. Association for Coaching's *Coaching Perspectives* magazine, April 2023, Issue 37, p. 42.

Moon, J. (1999). *Reflection in Learning and Professional Development*. London: Kogan Page.

Niemec, R. M. & McGrath, R. E. (2019). *The Power of Character Strengths*. Cincinnati, OH: VIA Institute on Character.

Peterson, C. & Seligman, M. (2004). *Character Strengths and Virtues: A Handbook and Classification*. Oxford: Oxford University Press.

Pressfield, S. (2012). *The War of Art: Break through the Blocks and Win Your Inner Creative Battles*. New York: Black Irish Entertainment.

Proctor, B. (2008). *Group Supervision: A Guide to Creative Practice*. 2nd edn. London: Sage.

Revans, R. W. (1982). What is action learning? *Journal of Management Development 1*(3): 64–75.

Robbins, T. (1980). *Still Life with Woodpecker*. New York: Bantam Books.

Robinson, K. (2001). *Out of Our Minds: Learning to Be Creative*. Oxford: Capstone Publishing.

Rogers, J. (2007). *Sixteen Personality Types – At Work in Organisations*. London: Management Futures Ltd.

Schön, D. (2016). *The Reflective Practitioner: How Professionals Think in Action*. Abingdon: Routledge.

Schwartz, S. H. (2012). An overview of the Schwartz theory of basic values. *Online Readings in Psychology and Culture 2*(1).

Sheather, A. (2019). *Coaching Beyond Words: Using Art to Deepen and Enrich Our Conversations*. Abingdon: Routledge.

Sheather, A. (2023). Creative Reflective Practice: A Guide to Creative Reflective Art Journaling. Association for Coaching Diploma in Art-based Coaching course materials.

Sibbet, D. (2010). *Visual Meetings: How Graphics, Sticky Notes and Idea Mapping Can Transform Group Productivity*. Mahwah, NJ: Wiley.

Tan, C., Chuah, C., Lee, S. & Tan, C. (2021). Being creative makes you happier: The positive effect of creativity on subjective wellbeing. *International Journal of Environmental Research into Public Health 18*(4): 7244.

Watts, A. (2022). *Collage as a Creative Coaching Tool: A Comprehensive Resource for Coaches and Psychologists*. Abingdon: Routledge.

Wheatley, M. (2006). *Leadership and the New Science*. San Francisco, CA: Berrett-Koehler.

Wheeler, S. & Leyman, T. (2024). *Playfulness in Coaching: Exploring Our Untapped Potential through Playfulness, Creativity and Imagination*. Abingdon: Routledge.

Whittington, J. (2020). *Systemic Coaching and Constellations: The Principles, Practices and Application for Groups, Teams and Individuals*. 3rd edn. London: Kogan Page.

# INDEX